The Geography of *Beowulf*

Map from *Medieval English Literature*, edited by J. B. Trapp, in *The Oxford Anthology of English Literature*, volume 1, under the general editorship of Frank Kermode and John Hollander, copyright © 1973 by Oxford University Press, Inc., reproduced by permission of the publisher.

(After Fr. Klaeber, *Beowulf*)

A READABLE *Beowulf*

The Old English Epic
Newly Translated

By Stanley B. Greenfield
With an Introduction by Alain Renoir

Southern Illinois University Press
Carbondale and Edwardsville

Copyright © 1982 by the Board of Trustees
Southern Illinois University

Printed in the United States of America
Edited by Stephen W. Smith
Designed by Design for Publishing

Library of Congress Cataloging in Publication Data
Main entry under title:

A readable *Beowulf.*

  Bibliography: p.
  I. Greenfield, Stanley B.   II. Renoir, Alain.
III. Title.
PR1583.G73   829'.3   81-16933
ISBN 0-8093-1059-7   AACR2
ISBN 0-8093-1060-0 (pbk.)

90 89 88   7   6   5   4

To *Tamma*

Contents

Preface

This volume has been a labor of love, a climax to some thirty years of research in and teaching of *Beowulf*. What I have produced is simultaneously a poem and, by virtue of the nature of translation, an act of criticism; it is also my testament of critical faith to the enduring value of the Old English masterpiece.

I cannot begin to give credit to all those who have contributed in one way or another to this re-creation of the Anglo-Saxon poet's epic vision, but mention of some of them is in order. First, I should like to pay homage to my now-deceased mentor and friend, Arthur G. Brodeur, without whose inspiration my scholarly feet might never have been directed to the *Beowulf*ian path. Then, I wish to thank the many students and colleagues, here and abroad, who have listened with patience and good nature to my ideas about translation and parts of my performance in countless classes and lectures over the last five years: their encouragement has sustained me often in the desert of my doubts. Particular thanks are due to Eric G. Stanley, who has probably forgotten that it was he who first urged me to try my wings in the rarefied air of poetic translation; to Peter Clemoes and Emmanuel College, Cambridge, who, through a Visiting Fellowship in spring 1979, furnished time and audience for a prolonged effort in the translative atmosphere; and to Daniel G. Calder, who, in reading the manuscript for the Press, helped bring

my flight of poetic fancy safely back to terra firma. I owe special debts to Alain
Renoir and Sarah Higley: to the latter, for her creative illustrations which mediate
so marvelously between the Old English poet's original vision and my re-created
version; to the former, for his introductory setting which brilliantly displays the
many facets of the Old English gem and for his continuing support, particularly
during spring 1981 when, as a visiting professor at his *gifstol* at the University of
California at Berkeley, I received his largesse. Finally, to my family for the help
that was *ofer min gemet* "beyond my measure": to my wife Thelma, for her "good
ear" and always insightful and diplomatic comments, especially on the "Translation" essay; to my son Sayre, for providing a humorous perspective on myself and
my magnum opus with his parodic "*Beowulf* among the Anapests"; and to my
daughter Tamma, to whom this volume is dedicated: she read an entire draft of
the translation and unfailingly pinpointed those spots where I flagged somewhat
in sound, rhythm, or clarity.

STANLEY B. GREENFIELD

Eugene, Oregon
September 1981

A READABLE *Beowulf*

Introduction

BY ALAIN RENOIR

The Old English poem which we call *Beowulf* after the name of its principal character occupies a special place in the history of literature. In addition to being generally recognized as the earliest substantial masterpiece of English secular poetry, it is the earliest full-length heroic epic to have survived in any Germanic language, and its contents make it almost mandatory to the historical study of several otherwise separate literatures. The only known version is in the West Saxon (i.e., from southwestern England) dialect but is usually considered a copy of a lost Anglian or Mercian (i.e., from northern or central England) original assigned by a great many scholars to the eighth century and by some to dates as recent as the tenth. It has come down to us in a tenth-century section of Manuscript Cotton Vitellius A.XV, at the British Museum, and in two copies made in 1786–87, at a time when the process of deterioration started by a fire in 1731 was less serious than it has since become. In the manuscript, which is devoted to pieces in Old English, the poem is preceded by three prose pieces—a fragment of the

A different version of this introduction was printed under the title of "*Beowulf: A Contextual Introduction to Its Contents and Techniques*" in Felix J. Oinas, ed., *Heroic Epic and Saga: An Introduction to the World's Great Folk Epics* (Bloomington: Indiana Univ. Pr., 1978), pp. 99–119. Indiana University Press was kind enough to allow entire sections to be reprinted here almost untouched.

legend of Saint Christopher, a text of *The Wonders of the East*, and a so-called letter of Alexander to Aristotle; and it is followed by a fine poetic version of the apocryphal Book of Judith.

These facts are of interest to the modern reader approaching *Beowulf* for the first time, since they suggest that the medieval monks who presumably compiled the collection at a time when the poem was still a modern work were perhaps not so concerned as we are with differences between genres or contents. Because it seems quite conceivable that this apparent lack of concern may have been in keeping with authorial intent and audience response, we have to accept the possibility that Old English schemes for literary classifications may have been quite unlike our own and that we might accordingly do well to unburden ourselves of modern misconceptions if we expect to experience the poem and appreciate what is there rather than vainly searching for what was never intended to be.[1]

The text of the medieval manuscript is divided into forty-three sections irregularly numbered in Roman numerals; it is printed as 3,182 lines of verse in a conventional modern edition, but, in keeping with Old English scribal practice, it has been recorded like prose without regard for individual metrical units. The following outline arbitrarily stresses those elements which will prove relevant to the subsequent discussion. Line numbers corresponding to key words and passages are listed between parentheses. For the sake of convenience, these and similar references throughout this introduction are to Stanley B. Greenfield's translation and may accordingly differ slightly from their counterparts in standard editions and other translations of the poem, and the same principle applies to the modernized forms of names found in *Beowulf*. Direct quotations are likewise from the Greenfield translation, except in the section devoted to the oral-formulaic nature of individual metrical units, where it has seemed advisable to preserve the Old English word order regardless of how much it might clash with modern English syntax. References to the Old English text are to the edition by Friedrich Klaeber which Greenfield used and which is included in the Selected Bibliography provided in the present volume.

1. For the advisability of keeping in mind the manuscript context of the Old English texts which we read, see Fred C. Robinson's compelling essay, "Old English Literature in Its Most Immediate Context," in John D. Niles, ed., *Old English Literature in Context* (Totowa, N.J.: Rowman and Littlefield, 1980), pp. 11–29.

Outline of Contents

The action of *Beowulf* takes place in Scandinavia. After an initial account of the founding of Denmark's Scylding dynasty by the mythological Scyld Scefing (1–52), the narrative traces the royal succession down to King Hrothgar, who decides to advertise the might of his realm by erecting near the modern town of Lejre a magnificent hall which he names Heorot (78–79). Here, king and warriors spend much time feasting at night until a troll-like and cannibalistic creature of darkness named Grendel (102), descended from Cain (107), takes such vehement exception to the constant revelry that he submits the hall to a series of murderous attacks which end all nightly occupancy by human beings for the next twelve years (147). Apparently nonplussed by the monster's irresistible savagery, Hrothgar finds no better solution than to bear his grief (147–49) and hold apparently fruitless meetings with his advisors (171–74).

Somewhere in the land of the Geats—presumably the modern Östergötland—a physically powerful young man identified as a retainer of King Hyglac (194–98), whose name we shall later learn to be Beowulf (343), hears of this situation and immediately sets sail for Denmark with fourteen companions (207–8) to free the Danes from Grendel's depredations. The Geats make land the next day and are challenged by a coast guard whose confidence they must earn before he offers to be their guide. Then, with the boarlike crests of their helmets shining in the sun (303–5), they march to Heorot, where Beowulf announces the purpose of his visit and his determination to fight Grendel alone and without weapons (435–39), though he will wear a corselet made by the legendary smith Weland himself (455). Hrothgar invites the Geats to sit at a banquet, during which Beowulf is in turn taunted by a retainer named Unferth (506–28) and honored by Queen Wealhtheow's gracious attention (620–27). The Geats are then left alone to wait for Grendel, who soon breaks into the hall and succeeds in devouring one of them before grappling for life with Beowulf, from whom he escapes mortally wounded, leaving an arm behind (815–36).

The next day, after following Grendel's tracks to his lake home in the fens, Geats and Danes ride back to Heorot, at times racing their horses and at other times listening to a poet compose and recite a poem about Beowulf's exploit

(871–74), which he likens by implication to the marvelous deeds of the Germanic heroes Sigmund and Fitela (874–900) and contrasts with the crimes of a wicked king of old named Heremod (901–15). During the sumptuous banquet which follows, Hrothgar bestows priceless gifts upon Beowulf (1020–45), and the poet performs once again, telling of the death of Finn and Hnæf (1063–1159) before Wealhtheow presents Beowulf with a necklace as valuable as the one which Hama once stole from Ermanric (1195–1201). That night, a contingent of Danes remains in Heorot, but Grendel's mother attacks them to avenge her son and carries off a warrior named Ashere, who is Hrothgar's dearest companion (1294–99).

Early the next morning, Beowulf is asked to help with the new peril (1376–77) and is taken to the lake where Grendel and his mother presumably have their lair and on whose shore he receives a valuable and tried sword from Unferth, who has now forgotten his earlier antagonism (1455–72). He dives into the lake, where he is seized by Grendel's mother and dragged into her underwater cave. Although Unferth's weapon fails him (1522–28), Beowulf finds an ancient sword which seems to have been waiting for him there, with which he kills Grendel's mother near the body of her dead son (1557–68). Back in Heorot, his accomplishments are praised by Hrothgar, who again contrasts him to Heremod (1709), and seizes upon the occasion to deliver a little sermon on the sins of pride, sloth, and covetousness (1724–68). On the fourth day, the Geats sail back to their homeland, where Beowulf's lord and uncle Hyglac expresses some surprise at the success of the expedition (1992–97). Beowulf tells Hyglac a slightly different version of his adventures, mentions that Hrothgar has promised his daughter Freawaru in marriage to Ingeld (2024–25), and gives Hyglac and his queen some of the gifts which he previously received in Heorot (2152–76).

We now learn that Beowulf was considered somewhat worthless in his youth (2183–88), and the narrative then jumps over half a century to a time when he has been king of the Geats for fifty years (2209). When a dragon, enraged at the theft of part of a treasure which he has been guarding (2214–31), begins spewing fire at the Geats and their dwellings and burns down the royal residence (2302–27), Beowulf decides to seek him out with a small band (2345–47). The narrative flashes back to Hyglac's death on a battlefield in the Rhineland (2354–9), his son Heardred's death at the hands of the Swedish king Onela (2379–88), and Beowulf's subsequent accession to the throne (2389–90), and back again to the occasion when Beowulf hugged a Frankish warrior to death during Hyglac's last battle (2502–8).

In front of the dragon's lair, the aged Beowulf now addresses the eleven retainers who have accompanied him and orders them to keep away from a fight which he describes as nobody's responsibility but his own (2532–35). As the fight begins and Beowulf's sword once again fails him (2575–80), his retainers run for cover to a nearby grove, with the exception of his younger kinsman Wiglaf, who gives them a brief lecture on the nature of duty toward one's lord and comes to his king's rescue in time to help him slay the monster (2694–708). Beowulf, however, has been mortally wounded (2711–15). He dies thanking God that he has been able to win the dragon's treasure for his people, asking that a barrow be erected for his ashes, and bidding Wiglaf to continue acting in a manner befitting the last of their family (2794–820). Wiglaf has the event announced to the Geatish nation by a messenger who predicts forthcoming trouble, possibly from the Franks and Frisians, and more certainly from the Swedes (2910–13, 2922–23), reviews the Geatish raid in the Rhineland (2913–21) and the Swedish King Ongentheow's killing of Hyglac's brother Hæthcyn at the battle of Ravenswood (2923–30) before falling at the hands of one of Hyglac's retainers (2977–81), and finally warns that the Swedes will set out against the Geats as soon as they hear of Beowulf's death (2999–3003). The poem comes to an end by the sea, on a promontory where a woman sings a song of sorrow (3150–51) by Beowulf's barrow, around which twelve mounted retainers mournfully ride while chanting a lament for their dead lord, whom they praise as the mildest, the gentlest, the kindest to his people, and the most eager for fame of all the kings in the world (3169–82).

Organization

Sketchy though it be, this outline illustrates some important aspects of the organization of *Beowulf* and the manner in which it handles time and history. We note, for instance, that three major principles of organization operate in the poem: from the point of view of emotional intensity, *Beowulf* divides into three sections centering in turn upon each of the hero's mortal fights against Grendel, Grendel's mother, and the dragon respectively; from the point of view of chronology, it divides into two sections centering in turn upon the hero's daring adventures as a young man and his exemplary deeds as an old king; from the point of view of narrative sequence, it again divides into three parts centering in turn upon the hero's adventures in Denmark, his own account of these adventures, and his deeds as king of the Geats. We also note that, with the exception of a few reminiscences and allusions by various members of the cast, the section concluding with Beowulf's return from Denmark to his homeland handles time in a basically linear manner, so that we need never question the chronology of the events which unroll before us. In contrast, the remainder of the poem repeatedly plays upon our sense of time by intermingling past, future, and present, as when both Beowulf's past exploits and the future catastrophes resultant from his death are brought to bear upon his present sacrifice to impress us with the tragic dignity of the event. In some of its most extreme manifestations, this aspect of the organization has been compared to the interlace designs much admired in the English art of the seventh and eighth centuries.[2]

Finally, we note the functional interweaving of legitimate history with what we are wont to dismiss as folklore or mythology. On the one hand, the eponymous founder of the Scylding dynasty belongs to the latter category because we have no accredited record of Scyld's existence, as does Beowulf for the same reason; and Grendel, his mother, and the dragon join them there because we do not believe in monsters. On the other hand, Heremod gets credit as a probable member of a royal line preceding that of the Scyldings, and Hrothgar clearly belongs in the former category because historical sources have led us to believe in his existence and to locate his death about A.D. 525. The same thing holds true of Ingeld, who married Freawaru about A.D. 518, of Hyglac, who triumphed at the same battle of Ravenswood where Ongentheow and Hæthcyn lost their lives about A.D. 510, and of the raid in the Rhineland during which Hyglac was killed about A.D. 521. We also have evidence for the existence of Heorot, which was burnt to the ground about A.D. 520, and for Onela's invasion of Geatish territory and his killing of Heardred about A.D. 533, as well as for other characters and events in the poem which have been left out of this outline. Like much early medieval history,

---

2. See John Leyerle, "The Interlace Structure of *Beowulf*," *University of Toronto Quarterly*, 37 (1967), 1–17, and Lewis E. Nicholson, "The Art of Interlace in *Beowulf*," *Studia Neophilologica*, 52 (1980), 237–49.

the evidence is open both to question and to interpretation, and, in addition, it seems to have been successfully manipulated by the poet for artistic purposes,[3] but it is solid enough to suggest a degree of historicity behind a fair portion of the materials in *Beowulf* and to help us locate the action within the context of the sixth century.

Traditional and Oral-Formulaic Features

Assumptions are always risky business when they concern a long-dead tradition of secular poetry whose preservation must perforce have depended upon the selective goodwill of the monastic scriptorium, and they are even riskier when the written records have been so thinned out by successive confrontations with the Scandinavians, the Normans, and the Reformation as to lead us into accepting views necessarily based upon a pitifully small number of surviving texts. Understandably, the bulk of Old English poetic materials which have come down to us is of a religious nature, but there are nevertheless grounds for assuming that a rich tradition of secular epic poetry must have been alive in England before the Norman Conquest. Besides *Beowulf,* for instance, we have fragments of two heroic poems dealing respectively with the bloody conflict between the forces of the Danish king Hnæf and those of his Frisian brother-in-law, Finn, and with the adventures of Walter of Visigothic Aquitaine; and the availability of the Medieval-Latin *Waltharii Poesis* enables us to surmise about the form and contents of the latter. In addition, scholars have argued the probability of an Old English original for the German *Hildebrandslied* and have tried to connect certain Old English poems with hypothetical heroic cycles devoted to Odoacer and to Offa. Finally, we have no reason to doubt the facts cited by Alcuin in a famous letter dated A.D. 797, where he admonishes the bishop of Lindisfarne to stop banqueting Christian priests from listening to poetry about the pagan king Ingeld.[4]

3. See especially Stanley B. Greenfield, "Geatish History: Poetic Art and Epic Quality in *Beowulf,*" *Neophilologus,* 47 (1963), 211–17.
4. For the text of the Finn-Hnæf fragment, see Friedrich Klaeber, ed., *"Beowulf" and "The Fight at Finnsburg,"* 3rd ed. (Boston: Heath, 1950), pp. 245–47; for the Walter fragment, see Frederick Norman, ed., *Waldere* (London: Methuen, 1933); for the *Waltharii Poesis,* see Karl Langosch, ed., *Wal-*

For the student of poetry, the wording of Alcuin's letter is as important as the contents. Not only does the text argue that the words of God are what ought to be read aloud whenever priests feast together, but it specifies that *someone who reads* ought to be heard instead of *someone who plays a string instrument* and that the sermons of the Church Fathers should be heard instead of local *songs* of presumably heathen origin ("Ibi decet *lectorem* audiri, non *citharistam*; sermones patrum, non *carmina* gentilium"). The contrast here is not only between the sacred and the profane but also between the written and the oral, between what is actually read from a book and what is sung to the tune of a musical instrument.

Assuming Alcuin to have been in control of both his vocabulary and his evidence, we may suppose that some Old-English narrative poetry was sung by musical performers who dispensed with the use of written materials. This supposition finds corroboration in Bede's *Historia Ecclesiastica Gentis Anglorum*, where we read that an untutored lay brother named Cædmon was divinely inspired to compose poetry after long years of running out in the middle of beer parties for shame of exposing his ineptitude whenever his turn would come to play music and sing his own compositions.

Students of literature will recall that Cædmon eventually became the first great English narrative poet still known by name today, and the fact that he performed orally may be inferred from the statement that his poems were taken down in writing by others. That Bede's account refers to the oral composition rather than to the mere recitation of set texts, and that it was construed accordingly by its intended audience, may likewise be inferred from the wording of the assertion that he was inspired to *make* poetry ("carmina . . . *facere*"), which the Old English translation of the *Historia* renders with an exact equivalent ("leoð *wyrcan*").[5] These observations necessarily raise a question about the means whereby

tharius, Ruodlieb, Märchenepen (Basel: Benno Schwabe, 1956), with face-to-face German translation, and English translation in Francis P. Magoun, Jr., and Hamilton M. Smyser, *Walter of Aquitaine: Materials for the Study of His Legend* (New London: Connecticut College, 1950). For the possibility of a lost Old English *Hildebrandslied* and for discussions of hypothetical Odoacer and Offa cycles, see Moritz Trautmann, *Finn und Hildebrand* (Bonn: Univ. of Bonn, 1903), Rudolf H. R. Imelmann, "Die altenglische Odoaker-dichtung," in his *Forschungen zur altenglischen Poesie* (Berlin: Weidmann, 1907), and Edith Rickert, "The Old English Offa Saga," *Modern Philology*, 2 (1904–5), 28–48. For the text of Alcuin's admonition, see Letter No. 81 in Wilhelm Wattenbach and Ernst Duemmler, eds., *Monumenta Alcuiniana* (Berlin: Weidmann, 1873).
5. For accounts of the string instrument and its function in poetic performances, see Jess B. Bes-

an oral poet might be able to compose a sustained and organized narrative of some length, be it at the request of a small group of scholars formally intent upon recording the performance or within the context of a less formal priestly feast or a totally informal beer party; and the scope of the question becomes obvious when we recall that at least one of the poems once attributed to Cædmon, the Old English *Genesis*, counts nearly 3,000 lines.

The most significant answer which the twentieth century has had to offer to the foregoing question is found in the theory of oral-formulaic composition, according to which the fully trained oral poet comes equipped with a stock of extremely flexible paradigms functioning at essentially three different but mutually supportive levels of composition to enable him to produce on the spot poems of various lengths with a controlled structure: 1) metrical and grammatical paradigms which make it possible to shape practically any sentence or part thereof into a proper metrical unit, 2) themes which act as paradigms for all kinds of situations and make it possible to select and organize metrical units into coherent narrative units often called type-scenes, and 3) larger traditional topics which make it possible to organize individual narrative units into an entire story whose duration may be adjusted to the expectations of the audience. To illustrate with a widely known, much studied, and readily available text, 1) practically any line picked at random from Homer's *Odyssey* is likely to conform to an oral-formulaic paradigm; 2) the scene, at the end of the thirteenth book, where Athena transforms Odysseus into an old beggar conforms to the paradigm of a traditional oral-formulaic theme whereby a returning hero is somehow expected to avoid immediate recognition upon reaching his destination; and 3) the entire *Odyssey* conforms to the paradigm of a traditional oral-formulaic story topic known as the return song.

The theory of oral-formulaic composition was formulated through the comparative study of Archaic Greek and oral South Slavic narrative poems, and it was subsequently applied to Old English narrative poetry. More recently, it has been

---

singer, Jr., "The Sutton Hoo Harp Replica and Old English Musical Verse," in Robert P. Creed, ed., *Old English Poetry: Fifteen Essays* (Providence: Brown Univ. Pr., 1967), pp. 3–26, and John Nist, "Metrical Uses of the Harp in *Beowulf*," ibid., pp. 27–43. The relevant sections of both the Latin and the Old English texts of Bede's *Historia* are conveniently printed in Frederic G. Cassidy and Richard N. Ringler, eds., *Bright's Old English Grammar and Reader* (New York: Holt, Rinehart and Winston, 1971), pp. 125–34.

tested through the comparative analysis of Old English poetry and Black African tribal poetry. The evidence demonstrates that the same poet can learn how to compose both orally and in writing, and the analysis suggests that some Old English lyrics—in contrast to narrative poems—could theoretically have been composed orally and that Old English oral poetry, or written poetry composed in accordance with an oral system, need not necessarily have been sung, as the proponents of oral composition used to assume.[6]

The foregoing outline is admittedly a gross oversimplification, but it should suffice to suggest that formulaic elements tend to be likewise traditional and that the theory of oral-formulaic composition can go a long way toward explaining the recurrence of certain similarities, both within the same texts and between separate texts whose shared features may not be attributed to a direct genetic relationship.

Although scholars continue to argue over the details, the intrinsic validity of the theory of oral-formulaic composition is generally accepted today. There is, however, a vast difference between recognizing the intrinsic validity of a theory, or even admitting its hypothetical relevance to a body of texts, and accepting it as the fundamental explanation for the form under which a specific work of the distant past was originally put together. As a result, most students of Old English would probably agree that Old English poetry exhibits the characteristics of oral-formulaic composition but that we have yet devised no reliable means of distinguishing an oral poem from a written one, and it seems probable that a poll on *Beowulf* would show that a substantial majority believe it to be heavily oral-formulaic but nevertheless composed in writing.[7]

6. Although the oral composition of poetry had received scholarly attention as early as the nineteenth century, the modern theory of oral-formulaic composition was first proposed by Milman Parry in 1928 (rpt. in Adam Parry, ed., *The Making of Homeric Verse: The Collected Papers of Milman Parry* [Oxford: Clarendon, 1971]) and subsequently developed by Albert B. Lord in his *The Singer of Tales* (Cambridge: Harvard Univ. Pr., 1960); it was first applied to Old English by Francis P. Magoun, Jr., in his "Oral-Formulaic Character of Anglo-Saxon Narrative Poetry," *Speculum*, 28 (1953), 446–67. For the implications of African tribal poetry, see Jeff Opland, *Anglo-Saxon Oral Poetry: A Study of the Traditions* (New Haven: Yale Univ. Pr., 1980). For the singing of Old English poetry to the tune of a harplike instrument, see Bessinger, "The Sutton Hoo Harp Replica," and Nist, "Metrical Uses of the Harp in *Beowulf*," in the previous footnote.
7. The case against accepting the presence of oral-formulaic elements as proof of actual oral composition has been argued by Larry D. Benson, "The Literary Character of Anglo-Saxon Literary Poetry," *PMLA*, 81 (1966), 334–41, and the general attitude of the scholarly world toward this prob-

Returning to the outline of the poem with these considerations in mind, we find that it illustrates some salient traditional and oral-formulaic features. Just as one of the heroic fragments mentioned earlier gives us tangible evidence of the fact that the bloody conflict between Finn and Hnæf was not our poet's exclusive property, so Alcuin's admonitory letter makes it probable that the deeds of Ingeld were in favor as topics for poetic performance in England at a time not far removed from that during which scholars believe *Beowulf* to have been composed. The extent to which the poem draws upon Old English literary tradition may be inferred both from these and from other names listed in the outline. Ermanric, for example, figures prominently in two poems, entitled respectively *Widsith* and *Deor*, which are generally considered highly representative of the heroic repertory of Old English literature. In addition, Weland—the same whose image on the Franks Casket may be seen by every visitor to the British Museum—plays an important part in the latter, while Hama, Finn, Hnæf, and Ongentheow are included in the former, where we also find Hrothgar's political situation described in a manner consonant with the account in *Beowulf*.

The most cursory and random glance at medieval German and Scandinavian traditional literature will show that the same kind of observation may be made in respect to the broader Germanic context. The Ermanric of the Old English poem is central to the German epic cycle of Dietrich von Bern and the Old Norse *Thidrekssaga* —both of which include Hama—and the sixteenth-century Low German *Koninc Ermenrikes Dot* makes it clear that the impetus of his fame was strong enough to carry beyond the Middle Ages. Weland also appears in the *Thidrekssaga* and rates an entire poem in the *Edda*. Sigmund and Fitela are probably best known as the central figures of the Old Norse *Volsungasaga*, and the latter's death is commemorated in a special prose link in the *Edda*, while the former is remembered as Siegfried's father in the Middle High German *Nibelungenlied*. The extent of their reputation is illustrated in the Old Norse *Eriksmal*, probably composed at Queen Gunnhild's request to glorify her husband, Eric Bloodaxe, who was killed soon after being driven out of Northumbria in A.D. 954: as the slain king enters Val-

---

lem has been discussed by Donald K. Fry, "Cædmon as a Formulaic Poet," in Joseph J. Duggan, ed., *Oral Literature: Seven Essays* (New York: Barnes and Noble, 1975). Stanley B. Greenfield, *A Critical History of Old English Literature* (New York: New York Univ. Pr., 1965), believes that Old English poetry was originally composed orally (p. 74) but inclines to think that *Beowulf* was composed in writing.

halla, the God Odin finds no more suitable means of proclaiming the magnitude of his heroic deeds on earth than to have him escorted by Sigmund and Fitela themselves. Sigmund, Ongentheow, Heremod, and Ermanric likewise appear in an Eddic poem, known in English as "The Lay of Hyndla," which also mentions the Scyldings.

In addition to these and other characters, important elements of the action in *Beowulf* find obvious echoes within the Germanic context, with close analogues to the first half of the poem occurring in the Old Norse *Grettissaga* and *Hrolfssaga Kraka* as well as in less widely known texts, and a fair analogue to the dragon fight occurring in Saxo Grammaticus's *Gesta Danorum*. We may therefore say that the contents of *Beowulf* are highly traditional and that the density of surviving attestations leads one to suppose that their tradition was alive and familiar at the time when the poem was composed.[8]

The oral-formulaic aspect of the poem is as obvious as its traditional aspect, though we must momentarily turn away from the outline and go to the text itself for an example of metrical formula. A glance at one of these lines will suffice to illustrate a fundamental aspect of the principle in question: "Beowulf spoke, the son of Ecgtheow" (1473: "Beowulf maþelode, bearn Ecgþeowes") occurs in precisely the same form, except for irrelevant spelling differences, eight additional times throughout the poem, and it obviously follows a pattern similar to that of "Hrothgar spoke, the protector of the Scyldings" (371: "Hroðgar maþelode, helm Scyldinga"), which occurs three times. We may thus conclude that we have here a verse formula whose grammar includes a) a subject proper name (Beowulf/ Hrothgar) followed by b) a verb conveying the utterance of speech (spoke/spoke) followed by c) a noun appositive (son/protector) and d) a possessive noun (of Ecgtheow/of the Scyldings), and which may be schematized as follows: *Y spoke + appositive noun + X possessive*. As long as the two halves of the line conform to a traditional alliterative pattern (as do "Beowulf/bearn" and "Hrothgar/helm" in the Old-English lines), we have a verse regardless of the actual words with which we fill out the schema; and the flexibility of the system is evident from the variant "Wiglaf spoke, Weohstan's son" (2862: "Wiglaf maðelode, Weohstanes sunu"),

8. The historical background and the analogues of *Beowulf* are succinctly discussed in the introduction and appendices to Klaeber's edition; detailed discussion will be found in Raymond W. Chambers, *"Beowulf": An Introduction*, 3rd ed., with supplement by C. L. Wrenn (Cambridge: Cambridge Univ. Pr., 1959).

which occurs twice in the poem and which switches appositive and possessive around in answer to the requirements of rhythm and alliterative pattern.[9]

An equally strong point may be made in respect to individual narrative units. Turning once again to our outline, for example, we find that the scene in which Beowulf and his Geats have just crossed the sea and begin marching toward Heorot conforms precisely to the paradigm of an oral-formulaic theme which often occurs before a reference to a mortal combat or before the actual performance thereof and in which a hero, in the presence of his retainers, at the outset or conclusion of a journey, usually near a beach or an equivalent thereof, finds himself within proximity of something shiny (in this case, the boarlike crests noted in the outline, of which the poem specifically says "Figures of boars, bright / and fire-hardened, gleamed gold-adorned / above the cheek-guards" [303–5]). Four additional occurrences of this theme have been found in *Beowulf* and many more in other Old English poems, while yet others have been discovered elsewhere, so that we have here a frequently attested and carefully studied oral-formulaic element which also happens to be one of many similar devices in the poem.[10] As may be expected, the presence of both themes and metrical formulas gives the texture of a poem a certain flavor which we do not normally find in the poetry of the modern industrialized world. This aspect of *Beowulf* must of necessity present a serious problem for anyone attempting to produce a translation into modern English which is at the same time readable and faithful to the original. The principles underlying the Greenfield translation are discussed in the essay following this one.

When used with the proper caution, the presence of these and other oral-formulaic elements may provide us tentatively with theoretical explanations for otherwise puzzling similarities between the Old English poem and some apparently unrelated works. Nobody reading such a close analogue to *Beowulf* as the *Hrolfssaga Kraka* is likely to experience much surprise at finding therein a counterpart of Unferth's taunting of Beowulf, but the reaction must surely be quite dif-

9. For studies of Beowulfian rhythms and alliterative patterns, see John C. Pope, *The Rhythm of "Beowulf"* (1942; rpt. New Haven: Yale Univ. Pr., 1966); Winfred P. Lehmann and Takemitsu Tabusa, *The Alliterations of the "Beowulf"* (Austin: Univ. of Texas Dept. of German, 1958); and Thomas Cable, *The Meter and Melody of "Beowulf"* (Urbana: Univ. of Illinois Pr., 1974).
10. The oral-formulaic theme in question was first identified by David K. Crowne in his "The Hero on the Beach: An Example of Composition by Theme in Anglo-Saxon Poetry," *Neuphilologische Mitteilungen*, 61 (1961), 362–72.

ferent when another counterpart turns up in the *Odyssey*, along with a counterpart to the scene in which Beowulf hears his own exploits turned into song by a poet. Here, the oral-formulaic theory suggests the possibility that both the Archaic Greek and the Old English poet may have used a common Indo-European theme extant in both the Hellenic and the Germanic poetic traditions.[11]

The story of Beowulf as a whole likewise conforms to the paradigm of a traditional topic known by students of folklore as the Bear's Son Tale and abundantly documented in European and other languages. It tells the story of a young man of superior physical strength who kills a monster in a strange place and tends to shy away from the use of weapons, as is the case with Beowulf when he wrestles Grendel and later a Frankish warrior, and as the poet emphasizes with the assertion that "it was his misfortune / that swords' blades were powerless to aid / him in battle" (2682–84).[12] We may therefore say that the mechanics and contents of the poem are in conformity with the principles of oral-formulaic composition, but it must be repeated that the experts are by no means in agreement about the actual mode of composition of the text as we know it and that the majority of them seems to incline toward written composition.

Pagan and Christian Elements

Another central matter about which the experts have been at odds for a long time is the juxtaposition of pagan and Christian elements. The temptation for disagreement on this point is hard to resist in a poem which draws on pagan mythology to offer Scyld Scefing, Fitela, and Sigmund as models of conduct but turns around to trace the monster Grendel's family line back to Cain (107 and 1258–67)

11. For thematic similarities between *Beowulf* and the *Odyssey*, see, for example, Albert B. Lord, "Beowulf and Odysseus," in Jess B. Bessinger, Jr., and Robert P. Creed, eds., *Franciplegius: Mediaeval and Linguistic Studies in Honor of Francis Peabody Magoun, Jr.* (New York: New York Univ. Pr., 1965), pp. 86–91, and Robert P. Creed, "The Singer Looks at His Sources," in Stanley B. Greenfield, ed., *Studies in Old English Literature in Honor of Arthur G. Brodeur* (Eugene: Univ. of Oregon Pr., 1963), pp. 44–52.
12. Klaeber includes a discussion of the Bear's Son Tale in the introduction and appendices to his edition of *Beowulf*, but the theory was developed by Friedrich Panzer in his *Studien zur germanischen Sagengeschichte, I: "Beowulf"* (Munich: C. H. Beck, 1910).

and threaten the warriors in Heorot with damnation for their failure to subscribe to Christianity (175–88). The ambiguity is compounded when the very same warriors who are threatened with damnation are seen listening to a song on the Creation (92–98) which sounds in nearly every respect like the first Christian poem attributed to Cædmon, and when their leader warns Beowulf against three of the Seven Deadly Sins (1724–78). It is further compounded by the contrast between Beowulf's code of honor and the nature of his funeral: just as the former, with the hero's insistence upon fighting his mortal battles alone, cannot fail to remind us of Tacitus's observation in *Germania* that the leaders of the ancient Germans were under constant obligation to demonstrate their superior courage and thought it utterly disgraceful to be surpassed in battle by anyone of their followers, so the latter, with twelve retainers and a woman mourning by their lord's barrow, cannot fail to remind us of the death of Jesus, especially if we happen to be reasonably familiar with the Old English *Dream of the Rood* and the Medieval Latin *Stabat Mater*. This juxtaposition of pagan and Christian elements, incidentally, is in keeping with the tangible lesson of archaeology. Although the seventh-century cenotaph found near Sutton Hoo in 1939 is best known to the general public for the wooden ship, the magnificent helmet, and the harplike instrument found therein, the remainder of the treasure counts both pagan and Christian objects, such as a whetstone presumably associated with the cult of Thor, nearby a bronze fish symbolic of Christianity.[13]

Because of these and other similar discrepancies, scholars have argued both the Christian coloring and the pagan coloring of the poem, in which they have both detected and rejected Christian interpolations into a pagan story and found everything between so-called essential paganism at one extreme and the story of Christian salvation at the other. It has been pointed out that the poet's pervasive concern for the union of wisdom and action may well be a key to this apparent ambiguity of allegiance, since the ideal of *sapientia et fortitudo*—to use the Latin formulation under which it has been generally known since the Renaissance—was shared by pagans and Christians alike and is found, for example, in the *Edda* as well as in Isidore of Seville's *Etymologiae*. Notwithstanding the logic of this argument, there is no reason to expect an end to what has thus far proved a lively,

13. For the contents of the Sutton Hoo cenotaph, see for example Bernice Grohskopf, *The Treasure of Sutton Hoo: Ship Burial for an Anglo-Saxon King* (New York: Atheneum, 1970), where the whetstone is pictured and discussed on pp. 79–82, and the bronze fish on pp. 83–84.

fruitful, and occasionally entertaining controversy, and students approaching *Beowulf* for the first time might do well to heed the sensible advice of a scholar who has pointed out that "we have no evidence that the *Beowulf*-poet intended that his poem be read as allegory, Christian, pagan or otherwise . . . , especially when the various symbols may depend upon fortuitous similarities not intended by the author himself."[14]

The Characters

However debatable the intended lesson and possible allegory, the subject matter of the poem is clear enough when considered from the point of view of an eighth-century English audience which was certainly not composed exclusively of literary critics and which may have been willing to accept poetic utterances at face value: *Beowulf* quite simply tells the story of a young man who becomes an old king, and it lets us see something of the process whereby he learns to conform to the ideal union of wisdom and action which is a necessary component of leadership.

Early in the poem, the aging Hrothgar is introduced as a wise and good (279: "frod ond god") king whose devotion to wisdom may be inferred from his holding apparently interminable meetings with his advisors to consider appropriate solutions to the problems presented by Grendel's nightly forays (170–74), but whose ability to act has so declined that he can only sit and wait (see lines 130, 177,

---

14. Michael D. Cherniss, *Ingeld and Christ* (The Hague: Mouton, 1972), pp. 130–31. The importance of the theme of *sapientia et fortitudo* has been argued by Robert E. Kaske in his "*Sapientia et Fortitudo* as the Controlling Theme in *Beowulf*," *Studies in Philology*, 55 (1958), 423–56; examples of the other views discussed above will be found in F. A. Blackburn, "The Christian Coloring of *Beowulf*," *PMLA*, 12 (1897), 205–25, where the theory of interpolations was first suggested, though it is now associated primarily with H. Munro Chadwick's *The Heroic Age* (Cambridge: Cambridge Univ. Pr., 1912), pp. 47–56; Larry D. Benson, "The Pagan Coloring of *Beowulf*," in Creed, *Old English Poetry*, pp. 193–213; Charles Moorman, "The Essential Paganism of *Beowulf*," *Modern Language Quarterly*, 28 (1967), 3–18; Maurice B. McNamee, S.J., "*Beowulf*: an Allegory of Salvation?" in *Journal of English and Germanic Philology*, 61 (1960), 190–207; Morton W. Bloomfield, "*Beowulf* and Christian Allegory: an Interpretation of Unferth," *Traditio*, 7 (1949–51), 410–15.

356, 1314) in deliberation or meditation when immediate action is obviously called for. As Beowulf has cogently argued in the course of his altercation with Unferth (590–97), this inability to act has in effect proved an encouragement to Grendel, who is basically all action. From the same point of view, however, Beowulf is almost as clear-cut a foil to Hrothgar as is Grendel. Whereas the wise old king is still attending committee meetings and debating what were best to do after seventy lines (100–169) of Grendel's murderous onslaughts, the young warrior needs only five lines (194–98) to hear of the situation and immediately begin doing something about it, by procuring a boat with which to sail to the rescue without giving a thought to the possible implications of his undertaking, as his uncle Hyglac is quick to remind him after the return from Denmark (1986–90). We may thus say that, as the story begins, Hrothgar is long on wisdom but short on action, while Beowulf is long on action but somewhat short on wisdom: neither conforms to the ideal of wisdom and action.

Like most unthinking men of action, Beowulf in the first half of the poem may appear unnecessarily brash and self-satisfied. Within the context of a society where good manners are so highly esteemed that an outstanding retainer is praised especially for his observance of the proper social behavior (358), we may be excused for questioning the young warrior's fitness for leadership when we hear him declaring publicly his intention to teach old Hrothgar how to deal with monsters (277–79), or trying to impress the assembled Danes with boasts of a martial reputation (419–24) which earlier, at least, the Geats had doubted (1990–97, 2183–88), or failing to realize his own arrogance when, in the presence of the experienced warriors who have thus far proved no match for Grendel's superhuman strength, he confidently proclaims his intention to overpower the monster alone and unarmed (424–26). These apparently youthful shortcomings contrast with Hrothgar's meticulously urbane answer, which credits Beowulf for his honorable intentions (457–58), acknowledges his own warriors' helplessness before Grendel (473–78 and 480–88), and suggests that God will easily solve the problem as He sees fit (478–79). Brash though Beowulf may seem to us, however, and even though the contrast pointed out here was presumably intended by the poet, we must not forget that his behavior earned him the confidence of the coast guard when the Geats first set foot on Danish soil a little earlier. Nor must we forget that the claims which he makes are in keeping with a tradition of boasting which has been recorded among Germanic people ever since 58 B.C., when Julius Caesar met Ariovistus and the latter opened the interview by bragging about his past deeds and those which he expected to perform in the future.[15]

Still, it is noteworthy that Beowulf wastes little time on any sort of reflection until the middle of the poem and his victory over Grendel's mother, even though the poet calls him "wise and brave" (825); and, even though we are told of his faith "in God's grace" (670), this faith seems by no means stronger than his trust "in his own great might" (670). His view of the world is simplified by the conviction that "fate must go as it will" (455), and his confidence in "his strength, / his hand-grip's force" (1533–34) as a solution to most problems is unshakable. As if in keeping with his boasting, his principal concern seems to be for the heroic image which he wants to project, and he accordingly dives into the monsters' lake with the assertion, "with Hrunting shall I / carve out fame, or death will vanquish me" (1490–91).

When Beowulf returns to Heorot after his victory, however, his tone shows signs of change: not only does he admit having survived the experience "not lightly" (1655), but his further admission that his "fighting days / soon had ceased had God not shielded" him (1657–58) suggests both his having given the matter some thought and his having learned to share with divine power the glory which is now his by right. In view of the number of mutually contradictory interpretations to which *Beowulf* has been subjected, one should exercise the greatest caution in assigning individual statements a place in a scheme which may or may not have been intended by the poet, and the admittedly artless reading presented here is by no means intended to invalidate more sophisticated analyses of the meaning of the poem. Its main point of interest, in addition to affording us an easy key to the action, is that it receives Hrothgar's own sanction within the narrative.

We have already noted how Hrothgar's polite answer to Beowulf's boasting implies faith in God rather than in any young upstart in search of renown, and it is relevant in this respect that his immediate reaction to the latter's victory over Grendel is to offer "thanks to Almighty / God" (928–29) rather than to the victor, whom he initially credits only with having acted "through God's grace and power" (940), before finally expressing the proper admiration for his fighting

15. For the interview between Caesar and the Germanic king Ariovistus, see Gaius Julius Caesar, *The Gallic War*, ed. and trans. H. J. Edwards (Cambridge: Harvard Univ. Pr., Loeb Library, 1970), pp. 68–77.

prowess by recalling how he has bestowed rewards upon many a warrior "weaker in war" (953). Now that Beowulf's account of his encounter with Grendel's mother hints at a newly acquired willingness to reflect upon a world where divine will may be more important than blind fate, and where physical strength alone may not prove a solution to all problems, not only does Hrothgar give him full credit for the deed, but he pays him the supreme compliment of praising him precisely for possessing the ideal combination of physical "strength" and "mind's wisdom" (1705–6) to control it and of predicting that he will become the support of his people (1707–9). In other words, Beowulf has now achieved much more than the purely martial fame which he claimed upon his arrival at Heorot, and Hrothgar is telling us that the apparently brash young man has matured into a thoughtful warrior worthy of assuming the leadership of his people if need be.

Hrothgar's judgment is amply vindicated by the remainder of the narrative, during which Beowulf becomes "a venerable king / and homeland guardian" (2209–10) after having shown enough commendable self-control to turn down an earlier offer of kingship (2373–76) and having wisely served his own young lord with "good counsel / and gracious friendship" (2377–78). Nowhere in the poem is this union of wisdom and action more obvious than in Beowulf's speech to his retainers as he readies for the dragon fight that will cost him his life. Here, we find none of the thoughtless bravado that marked his tone when he first announced to Hrothgar his intention to confront Grendel. Instead, we find reflection leading to a quiet determination to act in a manner befitting his position. As he refers to himself as the "old guardian" (2513) of his people, he makes clear his full awareness of both his royal duty and the difficulties which age has put in the way of his discharging it, and he accordingly determines to stand his ground and do battle "if" (2514) the dragon comes out of his lair to seek him. Contrary to his earlier practice (2518), he now carries a sword and feels the need to explain that he would not do so "if" (2519) he knew how else to deal with a dragon. Long ago in Heorot, he had already used the conjunction *if*, but he had done so in a boastful manner to suggest that Grendel might not dare (684: "if he dare seek war") meet him in combat. Now, on the contrary, the repetition of the same conjunction drives home the fact that he has weighed at least some of the alternatives before choosing the solutions on which he finally settles, and it lends the passage a reflective tone which is totally absent from his utterances in the first half of the poem.

Nor does he decide to fight alone in a reckless attempt to prove his martial valor before the world, as he did years ago with Grendel: though scholars have found a variety of plausible reasons for the deed,[16] the text tells us that he will fight alone quite simply because he knows that, as king and formal protector of his people, he alone bears the responsibility of meeting the unequal challenge, and he thoughtfully sets matters straight when he tells his retainers, "It is not your venture, / nor any man's measure save mine alone, / to match his might with the fearful foe's" (2532–34). In view of his awareness of the odds against him, his decision not to retreat by a single foot (2524–25) fully deserves the poet's admiring litotes: "such is no coward's way" (2541).

In effect, Beowulf has bridged the gap between foolhardiness and true courage in the Aristotelian sense. In so doing, he has raised his claim to fame above that of Hrothgar himself: like the old king in Heorot, he has learned to reflect and listen to the voice of wisdom before making decisions; unlike him, however, he has retained the will to act, so that he has become an embodiment of the ideal union of wisdom and action, and we have witnessed the process whereby the rather brash young man who enters near the beginning of the poem turns into the wise and formidable old warrior whom the conclusion praises as the best of all earthly kings. The foregoing observations, incidentally, are in keeping with J. R. R. Tolkien's view of the structure of the poem as "essentially a balance, an opposition of ends and beginnings. . . . an elaboration of the ancient and intensely moving contrast between youth and age, first achievement and final death," as well as with Greenfield's own illuminating perception that this balance "is emphasized further in the contrast between the *tones* of the two halves of the poem. The heroic dominates in the first part. . . . The elegiac dominates the second."[17]

Although there is no room here for the detailed discussion of secondary characters, a few words about Queen Wealhtheow are in order since she is the only woman with a significant part in this overwhelmingly masculine poem. What with her entering the narrative at line 612, leaving it at line 2174, and making numerous appearances in between, she participates in more of the action than anyone else except the principal actors, and her name is mentioned more often than any but six others, including Grendel's. As we see her hosting a great banquet in

16. For a list of arguments, see Greenfield, *Critical History*, p. 86, esp. n. 13.
17. J. R. R. Tolkien, *"Beowulf": The Monsters and the Critics* (London: Oxford Univ. Pr., 1958), p. 29; Greenfield, *Critical History*, p. 88.

Heorot, and strolling through rows of rejoicing warriors (611–12) to bring greetings and mead to Beowulf and others (620–24), her outward appearance shows all
the grace, cheerfulness, and poise befitting a great lady and the wife of a powerful
king. Her behavior both illustrates the function of a queen in Germanic society
and conforms to the expectations of the audience as we find it stated in the Old
English *Maxims*. There is another and more subtle side to Wealhtheow, however,
and it reveals itself in her repeated and seemingly unwarranted quest for reas-
surance concerning the future of her two sons (ll. 1175–87 and 1219–27).

Especially for those who happen to recall that, in actual history, her sons
never acceded to the throne and may have met with untimely and violent death,
Wealhtheow's concern adds to the feeling of insecurity which pervades the poem
as a result of strategically located reminders of the transitory nature of human
glory and happiness. No sooner has Heorot been erected, for example, than we
are forewarned of its eventual destruction by fire (82–83); no sooner has Beowulf's youthful vigor received full recognition for its triumph over Grendel's
mother and her son than we are reminded of the ravages which old age holds in
store for all of us before the unavoidable moment of death (1766–78); or no
sooner have we learned of Princess Freawaru's betrothal to Ingeld than we hear a
prediction of the disastrous and bloody outcome of that union (2029–69). In thus
alerting us to the elusive signs of an unstated but impending catastrophe, Wealhtheow not only contributes to the tone of the entire poem but illustrates something of the justified anxiety which mars the lives of nearly all the women of Germanic secular poetry.

Narrative Technique

The emphasis on the transitory nature of human achievements necessarily
yields an element of suspense, since we are constantly reminded that all the glory
of the world, and by implication all the good things toward which human beings
tend to aspire, must come to an ineluctable end whose time may not be predicted.
This element of suspense is intensified by the poet's masterful control of his technique, which finds ready illustration in his accounts of physical motion at key
points in the action. As the makers of horror films discovered long ago, the mon-

ster's slow approach is likely to prove far more suspenseful and terrifying than his sudden appearance on the screen, since it allows the audience to anticipate and share emotionally the fate of the intended victims.

Consciously or otherwise, the *Beowulf*-poet has composed in accordance with this principle, as we can see in his handling of Grendel's last raid upon Heorot (703–21). With the opening words of the passage, we are made to sense vividly the evil presence of some mysterious and destructive force of the night silently moving toward us as well as toward the Geats in Heorot, but we can only scan the darkness for the direction and distance whence it will reveal itself: "Out of dark night / swept death's shadow forward" (702b–3). Not until seven lines later is the approaching danger specifically identified as Grendel and its general location established with the statement that "Out of the moor then, under mist-hills, / Grendel glided, carrying God's wrath" (710–11), and the inexorable process goes on until the monster finally reaches his goal.

The mechanics of the passage have been submitted to an especially fine and revealing analysis in what is often considered the most important critical study of the poem: "It is a hair-raising depiction of death on the march. . . . Three several, *distinct* stages of the action are here set forth. This is not the familiar static trick of poetic conventions; it is dynamic and progressive. Each successive statement of Grendel's oncoming represents an advance in time, in forward movement, in emotional force; each shows an increase over the preceding in the use of horrific detail; each imposes increased strain upon the audience."[18] The strain is here for all but the most insensitive reader, and we need not have delved very deep into the mysteries of literary psychology to realize that it must have been even stronger with an audience for whom lurking monsters were altogether as real and difficult to control as air pollution and the dangers of radiation in the last quarter of the twentieth century.

The converse of this technique is used with equal mastery in the account of the march to the lake where Grendel and his mother have taken refuge. Whereas the passage discussed above forces us to endure the action from the point of view of the fixed target toward which the bloodthirsty monster is moving closer with every line, the march to the pond makes us participate in the action from the op-

18. Arthur G. Brodeur, *The Art of "Beowulf"* (Berkeley: Univ. of California Pr., 1959), pp. 90–91. For an elaboration upon Brodeur's analysis, see Stanley B. Greenfield's illuminating essay, "Grendel's Approach to Heorot," in Creed, *Old English Poetry*, pp. 275–84.

posite point of view as it takes us in pursuit of Grendel's mother along the mountain path leading to the dark waters (1399–1421), whose horror we have been made to anticipate through a previous account (1361–76). Like a traveling motion-picture camera, we accompany Hrothgar as he follows the monster's footprints until we reach the edge of the pond and come to an abrupt stop at the chilling sight of Ashere's severed head before shifting our focus to the chilling sight of blood welling on the water (1422–23).

The attention given to Ashere's head and the blood on the water brings up another aspect of narrative technique worth noting here. Like Stendhal, whose *Charterhouse of Parma* has impressed the battle of Waterloo upon generations of readers by focusing on bits of soil sent flying by cannon balls, the *Beowulf*-poet almost unfailingly comes up with the detail most likely to impress an entire scene upon our mind. When Beowulf leaves his homeland to seek Grendel, for instance, we are given no description of the ship which the Geats are boarding: instead, our attention is called to a single detail which sets our imagination working as we are told that, as the men were climbing aboard ship, "the waves beat / against the shore" (212–13). Elsewhere, as Grendel enters Heorot, we are again made to concentrate upon a single detail which is far more suggestive than any description of the monster himself could ever be: the "wicked gleam" (726) which shines from his eyes unto the pitch darkness of the hall where Beowulf is waiting in silence.

Perhaps as typical as the techniques discussed above is the extent to which *Beowulf* seems to call upon its audience to take an active part in the composition of the narrative. The device, which is probably as old as literature itself, requires the listener or reader to manipulate information drawn either from the text itself or from his or her own store of knowledge and to apply it to a framework designed by the author. In the novel, the modern period has provided us with a plentiful source of clear instances of the first alternative. Nearly everyone recalls reading one or more novels in which an unexpected piece of information provided by the author suddenly forces the reader to reformulate everything which has preceded it and thus participate retroactively in the creation of a literary artifact which is unlikely to be the same for any two readers.

In the *Aeneid* and the *Nibelungenlied*, Classical Antiquity and the Middle Ages have provided us with equally clear instances of the second alternative. When, in the twelfth book of the *Aeneid*, we find a crucial section of a council patterned upon a similar event in the first book of the *Iliad*, we are in effect invited to interpret the action in the light of unstated similarities and differences between the two situations, and we are cued in by the fact that the Latin word by which King Latinus refers to the scepter (*sceptrum*) on which he swears to maintain peace happens to be precisely the same as the Greek word by which Achilles refers to the staff (*skēptron*) on which he swears never to be reconciled to Agamemnon.

The same principle operates in the concluding section of the *Nibelungenlied*, when we are reminded of the time when Hagen passively sat on his shield while Walter of Spain massacred his companions. The reference is to an episode recorded in the *Waltharii Poesis*, where we find Hagen so hopelessly torn between conflicting allegiances that he can only look on and brood over his own impending loss of knightly honor while warriors to whom he owes equal support try to kill each other. When brought to bear upon the action of the *Nibelungenlied*, the information which we are thus invited to draw from an outside source forces us to reformulate our own view of Hagen's character only a few lines before we see his head roll under the sword of a vengeful queen.

Both alternatives occur in *Beowulf*, with the first one illustrated in Hyglac's surprise at the news of the successful cleansing of Heorot (1992–97), which prompts us to reconsider Beowulf's earlier assertion that he undertook the adventure at everybody's instigation (415–18); or in the poet's belated allegation that Beowulf had a "despised" (2184: "hean") childhood, which prompts us both to reconsider our hero's earlier boasting about his glorious youth (408–9) and to perceive a kind of structural relationship between him and the mythological Scyld Scefing, whose early childhood was also unglorious (7) but who nevertheless rose to the full glory of an ideal king and protector of the people. We may thus say that, like many a novel, *Beowulf* provides us with information which we are invited to manipulate in order to see certain key elements of the story not specifically mentioned in the text.

The second alternative is illustrated during the banquet in honor of Beowulf's victory over Grendel, when, at the conclusion of a brief account of the exemplary social behavior shown by Hrothgar and his nephew Hrothulf and of the atmosphere of friendship which fills Heorot (1011–18), we are suddenly told that the Scyldings had not yet performed "foul treachery" (1018). The statement stands out because its tone clashes with that of the festivities that are going on, because the information seems irrelevant to the immediate action, and because we find no justification for it in the preceding narrative. Precisely because it is so clearly out of place, however, it sends us searching through our own store of information, where we find what the poet presumably assumed to be common knowledge in his audience: upon Hrothgar's death in A.D. 525, it seems that the historical Hrothulf—the Hrolf of the *Hrolfssaga Kraka*—usurped the throne and presumably rid himself of the legitimate claimants.

Once properly impressed upon our mind, this and other similar reminders of historical facts outside the scope of the narrative become powerfully relevant to the immediate context: by keeping us aware that the glory before us is doomed to nought, they lend a tangible reality to the sense of transiency which pervades the poem; by keeping us aware that Hrothgar's sons will never succeed their father, they add tragic intensity to the concern which their mother shows for their future, as was suggested earlier in this essay. We may thus say that, like Vergil and the anonymous author of the *Nibelungenlied*, the *Beowulf*-poet cues us in to information which lies outside the text and which we are invited to manipulate in order to add a major emotional dimension to the narrative. These and the many other hints and allusions which invite us to join in the composition of the poem must have been especially effective with the original audience, at a time when much of what has since become recondite and uncertain history was presumably common lore, as obvious as a mention of George Washington's cherry tree is to most Americans.

The presence of the technique described above may possibly provide some explanation for the multiplicity of interpretations which have been noted earlier, and it certainly bears out the view that "there is no one key to the appreciation of *Beowulf*,"[19] for the fact is that there are probably as many versions of the poem as there are readers thereof. In addition, this technique tells us that, much more than a millenium after its composition, *Beowulf* remains a poem for active readers. Passive readers will find it a good story about a man who kills monsters, but those willing to follow the hints and allusions in order to participate actively in the composition of the story will find themselves sharing to the full in the joys and sorrows of human beings while experiencing the growth, the victories, and the death of one who has learned to recognize his own place in the scheme of things.

In view of the place of eminence which *Beowulf* occupies in the history of English literature, we must agree with a modern playwright, poet, and scholar

19. Kenneth Sisam, *The Structure of "Beowulf"* (Oxford: Clarendon Pr., 1965), p. 1. For a fine appreciation of *Beowulf*, see Edward B. Irving, Jr., *A Reading of "Beowulf"* (New Haven: Yale Univ. Pr., 1968).

who has called it "a national monument as well as a poem," [20] but one should add that it is a very special monument. On the one hand, it is a grand and monumentlike celebration of the ideal of human excellence; on the other hand, the way in which it involves each one of us personally and intimately in the action is as unmonumentlike as it is moving and effective.

20. William Alfred, trans., *Beowulf*, in William Alfred, W. S. Merwin, and Helen M. Mustard, *Medieval Epics* (New York: Random House, 1963), p. 9.

On the Translation

Though the *Beowulf*-poet composed in what was then known as English, the language has changed so radically in the thousand years since it was copied into Manuscript Cotton Vitellius A.XV that today only the specialist in Old English can read the original. Hence the need for translators. And there have been many who have sought to make the poem "readable" in the most basic sense of that word, turning this monument of Old English heroic literature into Modern English. But readability involves more than modernization, especially when the work in question is both a narrative and a poem. The fact that translator has succeeded translator (I furnish a list of most of the twentieth-century English poetic translators in the end matter of this book) testifies to the dissatisfaction each has felt with his or her predecessors' efforts to capture the literal meaning, narrative movement, or poetic qualities of the original. And here, in my turn, am I.

What do I offer that is better, more "readable" in all senses? Toward accuracy of meaning, the advantages of the intervening years' critical researches, including a number of my own published and unpublished reflections and enquiries. Toward reflecting the narrative cadences and aesthetic attributes—but I must pause before proceeding, and mention briefly some of the prominent features of Old

English or Anglo-Saxon verse, features which were the *Beowulf*-poet's stock-in-trade however uniquely he used them to tell his particular story.

Quite unlike modern poetic lines, the Old English verse line consists of two half-lines with two major or primary stressed syllables in each half-line; the number of unstressed syllables varies, within certain limits. The half-lines are "bound" by alliteration (initial rhyme), the third stressed syllable *always* alliterating with either one or both of the stressed syllables in the first half-line: for example, "*thé-odcýninga thrým gefrúnon*" or "*Oft Scýld Scéfing scéaþena thréatum.*" This verse line, with its marked medial pause (caesura)—indicated in modern editions by a large space between the half-lines—is also the Anglo-Saxon verse form since, with few exceptions, there are no paragraph or stanzaic divisions, and little end-rhyme. And the half-lines, and occasionally full lines, often contain oral-formulas, as Alain Renoir has made clear in his Introduction, in the section on "Traditional and Oral-Formulaic Features."

A striking feature of the narrative movement of Anglo-Saxon verse is its frequent interruption by restatement or multiple restatement of the same concept: a literal translation of *Beowulf* 129b–31 yields, for instance, "the famous prince, / the noble one virtuous of old, sat unhappy; / the mighty one suffered, endured sorrow for [the loss of his] thanes." Here we can see *variation*, as we call it, in both the grammatical subject (*the famous prince~the noble one~the mighty one*) and predicate (*sat unhappy~suffered~endured sorrow . . . thanes*); though single variation, such as in the formulas introducing speakers (e.g., *Beowulf~son of Ecgtheow*), is more common. Another striking poetic feature is a kind of metaphoric substitution for a simple word: "distributor of rings" for *king*, "heath-stalker" for *stag*, "cup of the waves" for *sea*. Such kennings appear more frequently in *Beowulf* than similes, though we have the marvelous image of the blade of the magic sword with which Beowulf kills Grendel's mother melting "into bloody battle-icicles; / . . . most like ice / when the Father releases frost's bonds" (1607–9). In addition to variation and kenning, the Anglo-Saxon poets used various small rhetorical patterns, like chiasmus: that is, an *a b b a* contour, perhaps subject-verb-verb-subject in a variation. They used also larger rhetorical patterns, like "envelopes," where a long passage begins and ends similarly; for example, the section where Beowulf arms himself for his descent into the mere begins "Beowulf dressed / himself in armor" and ends "once he had dressed himself for battle." And they "played" with sounds, with word associations, with double-entendre, even as modern poets explore and exploit such relationships between sound and sense. In *Beowulf*, for instance, it is surely not accidental that we learn that the name of the Geat Grendel eats is *Handscio* (meaning "hand-shoe" or "glove") precisely at that moment when we also learn that Grendel carried a glove or pouch into which he put his "meal in reserve" as it were (both pieces of information coming more than 1,300 lines after the event of the eating).

How does a poetic translator, desiring a readable *Beowulf*, handle such staples of the Old English poem? I shall not attempt to discuss what my predecessors have done, but rather simply clarify the principles and techniques I followed.

I wanted my translation to be not only faithful to the original but, as the late John Lennon would have put it, "A Poem in its Own Write." I wanted it to "flow," to be easy to read, with the narrative movement of a modern prose story; yet to suggest the rhythmic cadences, including variation, of the Old English poem. I wanted it both modern and Old English in its poetic reflexes and sensibilities, delighting both the general reader and the Anglo-Saxon specialist. For those who will listen to its sounds as well as see the words on the printed page—or, to paraphrase Shakespeare's Bottom, will use their ears to see and their eyes to hear—I wanted it to reproduce the intoxication of aural contours which, *mutatis mutandis*, might have pleased and amused warriors over their cups in the Anglo-Saxon mead-hall, or those monks in Anglo-Saxon monasteries who paid more attention to song and to stories of Ingeld than to the *lector* and the gospels.

A tall order! *Imitation* would not serve such ends; *equivalency*, I decided, would. I needed a verse form that was supple enough to allow the metrical freedom of modern poetry yet maintain a fixity suggestive of the four-stress, heavily caesured Anglo-Saxon line; and I had to use alliteration with greater subtlety than the Old English, since we are not so tolerant of that aural phenomenon. Word order had to be modern for both grammatical and rhythmic reasons, yet hew as closely to the original as was humanly possible. Fortunately, there was King Alfred's own precedent for translation: when that good king decided, back in the ninth century, that for his people's sake he had to translate some of the writings of the Church Fathers from Latin into English, he proceeded, as he himself indicated in his Preface to his translation of Gregory the Great's *Pastoral Care*, sometimes word-by-word, more often sense-by-sense within the syntactic or rhetorical unit. I have followed King Alfred's practice. I have also tried to use both modern stylistic and poetic techniques, weaving them where the seams will not show with

some of the Old English poetic features. This raiment of ancient and modern en-
tailed modification of formulaic repetition, kennings, variation, and the like, but
neither their total elimination nor mechanical retention. Two brief examples may
illustrate my methods. Lines 1136b–38a translated literally would be "Then was
winter departed,/fair earth's bosom; wished to hasten the exile,/guest from the
yards"; my version is "The winter was past,/earth's bosom fair: the exile fretted,/
a guest eager to be gone." The *exile~guest* is Hengest, in the Finn Episode. A few
lines later (1143–44) we would have literally (though there is some question of
meaning here) "when him [i.e., Hengest] Hunlafing the battle-flame,/of swords
the best, on lap placed," which I have rendered "when Hunlafing laid the best of
swords/which had flamed in battle on his lap." Unfortunately, I could not capture
some of the original's imagistic relationship in these two sections—between
earth's springtime quickening and Hengest's quickening desire for revenge:
"bosom" and "lap" are the same word in the Old English *Beowulf*, the word
bearm.

   But the difficulties of poetic translation and my attempts to solve them may
perhaps be seen more advantageously if we look at the opening eleven lines of the
poem: first in the original, following Friedrich Klaeber's great edition; then in a
literal rendition in which I indicate some of the ambiguities of meaning inherent in
the Old English grammar and words; and finally in my poetic version.

    HWÆt, WĒ GĀR-DEna   in gēardagum,
    þēodcyninga   þrym gefrūnon,
    hū ðā æþelingas   ellen fremedon!
    Oft Scyld Scēfing   sceaþena þrēatum,
5 monegum mǣgþum   meodosetla oftēah,
    egsode eorl[as],   syððan ǣrest wearð
    fēasceaft funden;   hē þæs frōfre gebād,
    wēox under wolcnum   weorðmyndum þāh,
    oð þæt him æghwylc   þāra ymbsittendra
10 ofer hronrāde   hȳran scolde,
    gomban gyldan;   þæt wæs gōd cyning!

What [Lo? Indeed?]! we of Spear-Danes   in yore-days,
of people-kings   glory have heard,

how then princes   deeds of courage performed.
    Often Scyld Scefing   from bands of enemies [with troops of warriors?]
from many nations [tribes?]   mead-seats deprived,
terrified warriors [Heruli?],   since first (he) was
destitute found;   he for that consolation experienced,
grew under clouds   (and) in honors prospered,
until him each   of those neighboring ones
over the riding-place-of-the-whale   obey had to,
tribute pay;   that was good [brave? excellent?] king!

In addition to the difficulties of ascertaining meaning, which I have indicated in brackets (the difficulty in line 6 depends upon a different emendation of the word "eorl" of the manuscript—to "eorle"), a syntactic question arises as to whether the word "syððan" in line 6 should begin a new sentence.
    Here is my version:

    Indeed, we have heard of the Spear-Danes'
    glory, and their kings' in days gone by,
    how princes displayed their courage then.
      Often Scyld Scefing shattered the hosts,
5 unsettled many a nation's mead-hall,
    terrorized tribes, since first he was found
    abandoned; comfort and abundance
    later came his way, and worldly fame,
    until neighboring nations, near or
10 far over whale-big seas, obeyed him,
    gave tribute; a good king in deed!

    The poetic line I have used is called syllabic verse, a pattern in which there are no metrical units or feet; instead, each syllable of the line receives equal stress. Syllabic verse has not been used much in English poetry, though some modern poets, including W. H. Auden and Marianne Moore, have assayed it. There is good reason for its scarcity: English, in its natural rhythm, is stress-and-unstress oriented. We cannot pronounce successive syllables without giving some relatively greater stress than others. Despite the fact that the reader of my lines will therefore naturally hear the syllables with more or less stress, my "fixing" of the number of syllables per line—I use nine, with occasional shortening to eight or expansion to ten—allows for the flexibility of modern poetry and simultaneously suggests the greater rigidity of the Old English verse line. My use of nine syllables instead of the more usual eight or ten of the modern English accentual unit line (as in iambic tetrameter or pentameter) produces more caesuras than we find in modern poetry; and though my placing of them is more flexible than the medial caesuras of the Anglo-Saxon, I think they create an equivalent effect.

With respect to alliteration, again I have tried for equivalency, not imitation. As I indicated above, I have felt the need for greater subtlety than exists in the Old English alliterative line. Often one of the alliterative sounds binding my line will fall on a syllable that has secondary rather than primary stress, as in the cases of "-*D*anes" and "*g*one" in my first and second lines, alliterating respectively with "In*d*eed" and "*g*lory." The alliteration in that first line is even less noticeable *to the eye*, since the primary stress on "Indeed" is on the second syllable. Frequently I bind sequent lines together with alliteration and other sound effects. Thus the "*d*ays" of line 2 picks up the "-*D*anes" of line 1; and "*c*ourage" of line 3 links with "*k*ings'" of line 2, both in sound and in sense. In line 3 "displayed" not only provides the *p* alliteration within the line (with "*p*rinces") but its *sp* sound links with that of "*Sp*ear-" in line 1. Line 4 comes closest to imitating the Old English pattern, with its "*Sc*yld *Sc*efing *sh*attered," since *sc* was pronounced *sh* in Old English. (On some matters of pronunciation, especially of proper names, see A Note on Pronunciation.)

The reader may also observe that lines 4–8 of the original have double alliteration in the first half-lines, whereas lines 1–3 have only single alliteration. While I have not imitated this sound contour for the block of lines, I have used equivalent devices. Let me point to only one, the assonance, consonance, and even the internal rhyme, as well as the alliteration, in line 8: "later came his way, and worldly fame." Rarely a line of my translation will have no alliteration; but I would note that any vowel alliterates with any other vowel in my version, even as it did in Old English practice: for example, "that no óther shíeld-béarer ány-where," line 858.

Admittedly, I have stretched the aesthetic contour of the original in this opening segment of the poem in several ways, perhaps most noticeably in providing an envelope pattern as well as a pun with my beginning "Indeed" and ending "in deed!" But both the envelope pattern and word-play of this sort, as I mentioned earlier, were part of the Old English aesthetic, and particularly part of the *Beo-wulf*-poet's aesthetic arsenal, and my translation legitimately conveys meaning embedded within the Old English image: for it is Scyld's deeds and those of his Danish successors that the poet is "hwæt-ing" as he begins his epic. The kind of enjambment in lines 9–10, "near or / far," and the echoing "tribes" and "tribute" of lines 6 and 11, are both modern and Old English in style. My lexical transformation of the kenning "hronrad" of line 10 into "whale-big seas" is both modern-sounding and expansive in its ambiguity, suggesting, even as the Old English does, the huge domain Scyld has built and, additionally, the birth of the Scylding dynasty.

That my nine-syllable line is capable of responding sensitively to differences in what we may call the density of the Old English poetic measures may be seen by comparing my lines 320–31, where Beowulf and his men march ringingly in their armor to Heorot, and lines 560–69, where Beowulf describes his fight with sea-monsters. Most lines in the former passage contain a relatively large number of stressed syllables (six, in one case: "hánd-wróught, glístened, and bríght íron ríngs") compared to those of the latter (in which in one line there are only two stresses: "they had no pléasure in my plénty"). Without going into technical detail about Anglo-Saxon verse measures, I would observe that the corresponding passages in the original reveal in the earlier passage a comparatively large number of heavy half-lines (that is, half-lines containing a secondary as well as primary stresses) and in the later passage a comparatively small number of such half-lines.

One particular challenge in capturing sound and sense I cannot resist mentioning here. In an essay entitled "The Ugly and the Unfaithful: *Beowulf* through the Translator's Eye" (*Allegorica*, 3 [1978], 161–71), Alain Renoir commented on the impossibility of re-creating in Modern English the precise meaning and aesthetic beauty of *Beowulf*; in particular, he analyzed lines 702b–5a, the famous lines which begin Grendel's approach to Heorot:

> Com on wanre niht
> scriðan sceadugenga. Sceotend swæfon,
> þa þæt hornreced healdan scoldon,
> ealle buton anum.

[Literally: "Came in the dark night 'shrithing' the shadow-goer. 'Shooters' slept, those who that gabled hall were supposed to guard, all but one."] Renoir, in partial support of his analysis, quoted an earlier article of mine, wherein I had suggested that part of the aesthetic delight, as well as the meaning, of the passage resided in the chiasmus of line 703, with its verbs at the ends and its nouns up against each other in the middle; and with the alliteration binding the shadow-goer, his action, and the object of his action across the medial caesura. Renoir also pointed to the problem of translating "scriðan" so as to catch its various meanings of "gliding," "stalking," and "striding"—all relevant here. Therefore I made a special effort in translating these lines to find an equivalent for all this in sounds, meaning, special effects.

> Out of dark night
> swept death's shadow forward. The warders slept,
> warriors set to guard that gabled hall—
> all but one.

I *shall* resist analyzing what I have done here! But I hope these few pages of explanation and analysis will be a gateway to some of the riches of the Old English epic I have tried to re-present in a readable and, I trust, delightful re-creation. *Bruc ealles well*: "Enjoy all well."

A Note on Pronunciation

In most cases I have kept proper names in their Old English form. *Sc* should be pronounced [sh], as in Scyld Scefing [Shild Shāving]; the *f* between vowels or between a vowel and a voiced consonant is voiced (so also are *s* and *th*). Initial *H* before consonants alliterates and should be pronounced: Hrothgar [Hrṓð gär]. Diphthongs count as one vowel and thus are part of the same syllable: Beowulf [Bā́ō wulf] is thus only two syllables. A *cg* represents the sound [dʒ] as in *judge*: Ecgtheow [Edʒ, thāō]. The hall Hrothgar builds is sometimes monosyllabic [Heort] and sometimes disyllabic [Heó rot], even as it is in the original. The name of the Swedish king Onela is trisyllabic [ón ə lä]. On the pronunciation of other names, see the Glossary of Proper Names.

Some of the common words vary in the number of syllables in their pronunciation, according to the syllabic dictates of the lines: words like *power* and *noble* may be one or two syllables; those like *warriors* and *curious* may be two or three syllables; those like *miserable* and *liberally* may be three or four syllables.

Beowulf

Indeed, we have heard of the Spear-Danes'[1]
glory, and their kings', in days gone by,
how princes displayed their courage then.

Often Scyld Scefing shattered the hosts,[2]
unsettled many a nation's mead-hall,
terrorized tribes, since first he was found
abandoned; comfort and abundance
later came his way, and worldly fame,
until neighboring nations, near or
far over whale-big seas, obeyed him,　　　　　　　10
gave tribute: a good king in deed!
To him in his homeland a young heir
soon was born, whom God by His grace sent
for his people's comfort: He perceived
the long distress they'd suffered lordless;　　　　15
the Lord of life, Ruler of glory,
heaped worldly honors upon Beowulf,[3]
Scyld's son, so that his fame spread widely
in Danish lands in his youthful days.
As he did, every noble youth should do:　　　　　20

Prologue: Scyld Scefing's Arrival and Departure

1. Spear-Danes] The Danes are called, further, Bright-Danes, East-Danes, North-Danes, South-Danes, West-Danes, etc. Other tribes or nations have similar compound names, the first element serving for purposes of alliteration, though some critics have suggested they may bear specific meanings in their local contexts.
2. Scyld Scefing] The *-ing* ending may, as here, probably, be a patronymic (Scyld, the son of Scef), or it may indicate a dynasty, as in *Scyldings*, or it may indicate a sword name, as in *Hrunting* and *Nægling*, among other things. Earlier critics associated Scyld Scefing with martial (shield) and agricultural (sheaf) gods. On the pronunciation of *sc*, see On the Translation.
3. Beowulf] So the manuscript, though most scholars now agree that the original name here was *Beow*. He is not the hero of the poem, but a Dane, the grandfather of King Hrothgar (see ll. 59–61).

spend liberally, give lavish gifts
while with his father, so that in turn,
when he comes of age, companions by choice
will serve him well when war comes; by deeds
25   worth praise will one prosper everywhere.
        At the destined time, still strong in might,
Scyld passed into the Lord's protection:
they bore him then to the ocean's brim,
his dear companions, as he'd commanded
30   while long as the Scyldings' friendly lord[4]
and prince he'd power over words and land.
In harbor stood the prince's ring-prowed ship,
outward bound to take its icy way.
They laid down then their belovèd lord,
35   the ring-giver who'd earned great glory,
in the ship's middle, hard by the mast.
Fine treasures from far-off parts were fetched:
never have I heard of any craft
so resplendent with the spoils of war,
40   with swords and coats of mail; in its midst
lay many treasures, to travel far
with him into the sea's dominion:
they lavished on him no lesser gifts,[5]
no meaner wealth, than did those men
45   who launched him forth in his life's first dawn,
a boy alone on the breaking waves;
further, they set high above his head
a golden ensign, let the sea take him,
gave him to the main with saddened minds,
50   in mournful mood. Men do not know how
to tell truly, wise men or warriors

4. Scyldings] I.e., the Danes.
5. Lines 43–45 constitute an example of the rhetorical device of litotes, a kind of understatement with ironic overtones, since Scyld had been found "abandoned" (l. 7) or destitute.

Sarah Higley

I   *The Establishment*
of the Scylding Dynasty

                    beneath the heavens, who received that load.
                        Then Beowulf long was belovèd king [6]
                    of the Scyldings, famed in the cities—
55   his princely father had passed away—
                    until to him in turn came Halfdane,
                    his great heir, who ruled the gracious Scyldings
                    till old, and ever bold in battle.
                    Four children followed him, the chieftain
60   of that host, as I have heard: they were
                    Heorogar, Hrothgar, and Halga the Good, [7]
                    and one was Onela's cherished queen, [8]
                    consort of the valiant Swedish king.

The Building of Heorot,
and Grendel's Attacks
                        Then good luck in war was Hrothgar's lot:
                    glory in battle came and kinsmen
                    gladly obeyed him, a band of youths
                    swelled soon to a mighty host. His mind
                    conceived a great hall: he commanded
                    such a mead-hall be built as would be
70   ever held by men in memory;
                    therein determined to distribute
                    to young and old all gifts God gave him,
                    except public land and people's lives.
                    Then I heard that many tribes on earth
75   from far and wide were ordered to work
                    to make that building beautiful; soon
                    it was finished, finest of great halls,

6. I] Roman numerals in the MS indicate sections of the poem, running from I to XLIII. These sections are called fitts; their exact contours have been the subject of much discussion. A few of the fitt numbers are not clearly designated; such are indicated in brackets.
7. On the Danish, Swedish, and Geatish dynasties, see Genealogical Tables.
8. The text is faulty; some scholars think the name of Hrothgar's daughter is mentioned here, and suggest *Yrse*. Onela reappears later in the poem.

in a short time. He whose very word[9]
was widely held as law called it Heort. — *Hrothgar's Hall*
Heort
He made good his vow: he gave out rings, 80
treasure at the feast. The hall towered[10]
high, wide-gabled, awaited the hostile *kin-killing*
surge of flame in battle, though the feud
of father- and son-in-law still lay
in distant time for dire hate to rouse. 85
        Then that powerful demon, he who dwelt[11]
in darkness, impatiently endured
a time of torment, hearing daily
loud joy in the hall, the harp's music,
the bard's clear song. He said, who could best 90
tell of man's ancient origin,
how the Almighty Lord made the earth,[12]
this wondrous land circled by water;
how He set in triumph sun and moon
as lights for those living on the land, 95
and adorned all corners of the earth
with leaves and branches; how He breathed life
into all kinds of moving creatures.
So that lordly band lived joyfully,
happily, until a hellish fiend 100
inflicted painful crimes upon them:
that gruesome demon was called Grendel;
he haunted the waste borderland, held
in fief the moors and fens and fastness.
The miserable man dwelt with monsters 105

9. Lines 78–79] I.e., Hrothgar. *Heort* (*Heorot*) means "hart," the royal beast.
10. Lines 81–85] An allusion to the later destruction of Heort in the feud between the Danes and the Heatho-beards—on that feud, see ll. 2024–69. It is mentioned also in the Old English poem *Widsith*.
11. I.e., Grendel.
12. Lines 92–98] Cf. the biblical account of creation in Genesis 1.

all the while, proscribed by the Creator[13]
among the kin of Cain, whose killing
Abel the Eternal Lord avenged:
Cain reaped no joy from that crime, for God
110   exiled him far from mankind for it.
Thence all wicked progeny awoke:[14]
ogres and elves and the walking dead,
and those giants who strove against God
a long time: the Lord requited that.[15]

II   115   When night descended, Grendel set out
to seek the towering hall, to see
how the Ring-Danes fared after drinking.
There within he found a troop of thanes[16]
asleep after the feast, unaware
120   of human care. That evil creature,
furious and greedy, grim and fierce,
at once was ready, and from their rests
ripped thirty thanes, and thence departed
homeward bound exulting in booty,
125   sought his lair with his feast of the slain.
Then in the dawn of advancing day,
Grendel's ravage was revealed to men;
then after feasting there was weeping,
loud morning wailing. The illustrious
130   prince, deserving good, sat dejected,
the mighty lord mourned the loss of thanes,
when they saw clearly the loathsome spoor
of the damned spirit: here was strong strife,
hateful and long-lasting! In no less

13. Lines 106–10] For the Cain-Abel story, see Genesis 4:1–12.
14. Lines 111–13] The linking of these evil broods to Cain probably
derives ultimately from the apocryphal Book of Enoch (I).
15. A reference to the biblical flood—see Genesis 6:6–24, and cf.
below ll. 1689–93.
16. thanes] I.e., retainers; those warriors who were closest companions to Old English and early Germanic war-lords or kings.

than one night he once again performed   135
more atrocious and murderous acts,
unrepenting of his evil ways.
It was not hard then to find the thane
who sought a more distant sleeping place
elsewhere in softer chambers when he   140
had such evidence of enmity
from *this* hall-thane: he who escaped
that foe kept farther off, more secure.
Thus he ruled and fought unrightfully
one against all, till that best of halls[17]   145
stood desolate. A long time things stood
thus: twelve years the Scylding's lord endured
such woe, more painful each passing one,
suffered dreadfully; and by sad songs
it became no secret to the sons   150
of men that for a great while Grendel
waged hateful war against King Hrothgar,
season after season persisted
on his sinful path, would make no peace
with any man among the Danish host   155
or cease from crime, pay compensation:[18]
no counselor had any cause for hope
of settlement from that slayer's hands!
But the dreadful foe, death's dark shadow,
kept on killing both the old and young,   160
lurked near and waylaid them, night after night
roamed the misty moors: a mystery
to men, the twists and turns of demons.
    So mankind's foe committed crimes,

17. Lines 145–46] I.e., the hall stands desolate at night, when Grendel, a creature of darkness, roams; cf. ll. 166–67.
18. Lines 156–58] Under old Germanic law, a victim's slayer could
only buy peace with the victim's kinsmen by paying a monetary
compensation called *wergild* ("man-payment"). Grendel, obviously,
has no intention of being subject to law.

165   the gruesome exile took grievous toll;
      he dwelt in Heort in the dark of night,
      making the hall, bright with treasure, his,
      though God kept him from the throne where gifts[19]
      were shared, and showed him no affection.[20]
170   Great anguish of mind and heartfelt grief
      distressed the Scyldings' lord. Strong men
      often sat in council, considering
      how warriors who had courage might best cope
      with his terrible and swift attacks.
175   At times in heathen temples they made
      offerings, prayed to the soul-slayer[21]
      for aid against the great and endless
      calamity. Such was their custom,
      the hope of heathens: it was hell that
180   governed in their thoughts, not knowing God,
      Judge of deeds and true Lord, nor justly
      how to praise Heaven's Protector,
      the King of glory. Unkind the fate
      of him who through cruel need must thrust
185   his sinning soul into the fire's embrace,
      have no hope for change! Happy the fate
      of him who after his death-day seeks
      bountiful peace in the Lord's embrace!

III   So Halfdane's son brooded ceaselessly

19. Lines 168–69] One of the famous cruxes of the poem; usually taken to indicate the sacrosanct nature of the royal throne and Grendel's inability, unlike a lawful "thane," to receive gifts from the throne; but the passage could be taken to mean that God was keeping Hrothgar from his own gift-throne during the nights, as part of the injury Grendel is being allowed by God to inflict upon the king.
20. showed him no affection] Another example of litotes; i.e., God reveals his anger towards *him* (whether Grendel or Hrothgar).
21. soul-slayer] I.e., the Devil; though the Danes are pictured as heathens here, as they historically were, Hrothgar speaks like a Christian, or at least monotheistic, king.

on that time of care; the wise warrior   190
could not dispel his people's nightmare,
set aside his woe: too distressing,
hateful, and long-lasting was that strife!

Beowulf's lord & uncle

    In his homeland Hyglac's thane, renowned [22]   *Young Beowulf Goes to*
among the Geats, heard of Grendel's deeds;   *Hrothgar's Aid*
he was in strength the strongest of men
who lived in that distant day and age,
awesome and noble. He ordered
a sound ship readied for the waves, said
he would seek the famous king, would cross   200
the sea where the swan rode, to give aid.
Wise men did little to dissuade him
from that deed, though he was dear to them,
but urged the bold man on, saw good omens.
The hero chose from the Geatish host   205
the bravest and the boldest champions
he could find; fifteen in all, they sought
the wooden craft; a sea-crafty man
guided their path to the coastal plain.
Time passed. And there lay the boat, afloat   210
under the cliff. The ready men climbed
aboard at the prow, while the waves beat
against the shore; into the ship's hold
they bore their gleaming battle-armor,
their splendid war-gear; the warriors launched   215
the well-crafted ship on their desired course.
Then over the waves, sped by the wind,
foam ringing its prow, the ship flew on
like a bird, till in time the next day
its curved prow had advanced to the point   220
where the seafarers could sight the land,

22. Hyglac's thane] I.e., Beowulf, the hero of the poem, who is not
actually named till l. 343. Hyglac is king of the Geats, and Beowulf's
uncle.

sea-cliffs gleaming, and the craggy bluffs,
the broad headlands. Behind lay the sea,
the crossing over. Quickly the Geats
225   sprang on to the shore and moored their ship:
as they moved, their coats of mail rang out,
their battle-garments sang; they thanked God
their ocean journey had been easy.

The Danish Coast   Then from the wall the Scyldings' warden,
Guard Challenges   whose task was to keep the sea-cliffs safe,
Beowulf   saw bright shields, battle-ready armor,
carried down the gangway. Curious,
he wondered who and what those men were.
So, riding his horse, right to the shore
235   went Hrothgar's thane; in his hand he shook
his great spear, spoke to them formally:
"What kind of men are you, armor-clad
in your coats of mail, who have thus come
hither in so tall a ship, taking
240   the sea-paths in your stride? For some time
have I guarded this land's end, held sea-watch
so that no foes with a force of ships
could launch a raid in our Danish land.
No other band has come so openly
245   with shields, yet you have no leave to land,
have not received consent of kinsmen,
our noble leaders. Never have I seen
such greatness as one of you suggests:
that warrior so worthily armed
250   is no plain hall-thane, else peerless looks
deceive. Come now: I must know the source
of your coming, and why, so that you'll
not be held as spies hastening further
into Denmark. Now mark well my thought,
255   you who dwell afar and dare the sea:
it were best for you to be in haste

to make quite clear whence you've come, and why."
      The group's leader gave him answer,   IV
disclosing rich thoughts with careful words:
"We are by origin of the Geats,   260
and hearth-companions of King Hyglac.
My father was a famous war-chief
well known to nations, his name Ecgtheow.
He lived for a long time before, old,
he passed away; throughout the wide world   265
wise men readily remember him.
With loyal heart we have come to seek
your princely lord and land's protector,
Halfdane's son; help us with your counsel!
We are here on an urgent errand   270
to Denmark's powerful king; I expect
nothing will remain concealed. You know
whether what we've heard is truly so:
that some fearful enemy descends
upon the Scyldings on dark nights, shows   275
mysterious hate, humiliates
and destroys them. I can advise
Hrothgar from a generous heart how
he, wise and good, can conquer that foe—
if ever any end to this evil   280
is to come, his cares find remedy,
and sorrow's surges subside and cool;
or always this time's tribulation
will be his, while that best of houses,
his royal hall, stands tall on its high place."   285
      From where he sat astride, the warder spoke,
a fearless officer: "Discerning
guardians of their land must learn to judge
empty words from words embracing deeds.
I believe this is a loyal band,   290
friendly to the Scyldings' lord. Go forth

bearing arms and armor: I'll be your guide.
Also, I will order my young thanes
to keep your new-tarred ship securely
295 on the shore against all enemies,
until that curved-necked craft once again
shall deliver you, belovèd man,
across the waters to Wedermark:[23]
such doers of good deeds will surely
300 pass through the storm of battle safely."
     They started out then—the spacious ship
remained behind, riding on its rope,
firmly anchored. Figures of boars, bright[24]
and fire-hardened, gleamed gold-adorned
305 above the cheek-guards: in war the boar
helped guard those fierce men's lives. The group
    marched
in step quickly, until they could see
the well-built hall shining bright with gold:
to men on earth no other building
310 seemed as splendid as this ruler's seat:
its light illuminated many lands.
The brave guide pointed out the bright hall
where bold men gathered, that they might go
right to it. Turning his horse around,
315 the warrior then spoke these words to them:
"It is time for me to go. May God
the Almighty grant you His grace to be
safe in your ventures. I'll to the sea,
to bear watch against marauding bands."

23. Wedermark] Beowulf's homeland, the land of the Geats, who are also called Weders or Weder-Geats.
24. Lines 303–6] Archaeological finds support this poetic description; the helmet in the famous Sutton Hoo excavation (see Introduction), for example, suggests that gilt boar-figures were placed in front of the cheek-guards for defensive purposes, both physical and magical, the boar being a totem figure.

The road gleamed with stones, the path guided   *The Geats Arrive*   V
the men together. Hard coats of mail,   *at Heorot*
hand-wrought, glistened, and bright iron rings
rang in their armor as they arrived,
reaching the hall in awesome array.
The sea-weary sailors placed their shields,   325
broad and massive, by the building's wall,
sat on the bench, iron resounding
in their gear; the sea-men stacked their spears,
which looked from above like an ash-forest
tipped with gray—the armed troop took glory   330
in its weapons. A proud warrior there[25]
then asked the champions their origins:
"Whence have you brought those gold-plated shields,
gray shirts of mail and helmets with masks,
this huge host of spears? I am Hrothgar's   335
herald and officer. I've not seen
so many strangers endowed so well.
I'm sure high daring and heart's greatness,
not banishment, brings you to Hrothgar."
The proud Weder-Geat, famed for his prowess,   340
hardy under helmet, answered him:
"We hold Hyglac as our lord, share feasts
along his bench; Beowulf is my name.
I have a message for Halfdane's son,
and would deliver it to your lord,   345
your glorious prince, if he will grant us,
out of his great goodness, audience."
Wulfgar spoke—a man of the Vandals,[26]
his mettle was well known to many,
his valor and wisdom: "As you wish   350

25. I.e., the door-warden, Wulfgar, named in l. 348.
26. Wulfgar probably comes from Vendel, in Sweden; like many
warriors of that time, he would have sought service abroad with a

I shall request of the Danish king,
the illustrious prince and Scyldings' lord:
ask the ring-giver about your errand,
and speedily bring you such response
355 as that good king sees fit to give me."
        He hastened then to where Hrothgar sat,
old and hoary, with his band of heroes;
known for valor, knowing court custom,
he went and stood by the ruler's shoulder.
360 Wulfgar addressed his dear friend and lord:
"Geatish men have made a journey here,
come from far across the ocean's course;
the bold challengers call their chieftain
Beowulf. They ask that they be allowed
365 to speak with you, my prince, to greet you
with warm words; give a welcome answer
to that mild request, o kind Hrothgar!
From their war-gear they seem most worthy
of the esteem of heroes; stalwart
370 indeed is he who led those men hither."

VI   Hrothgar, the Scyldings' guardian, spoke:
"I knew him when he was but a boy;
his father, Ecgtheow, won the favor
of the Geat king, Hrethel, who gave him
375 his sole daughter's hand; now his brave son
comes here to visit a valued friend.
Something else: our seafarers have said,
those who have carried gifts to the Geats
as pledges, that he, powerful in war,
380 possesses the might of thirty men
in the grip of his hand. I have hope
that of His grace Holy God has sent him

---

powerful king, out of a spirit of high adventure: hence the point of
his courteous comment in ll. 338–39.

here to us West-Danes to war against²⁷
Grendel's terror. Treasures shall I give
to that good man for his great daring.   385
Quickly, go and bid that noble band
enter all together to see us,
and in warm words say they are welcome
to the Danes." Wulfgar stepped to the door;
the warrior from within spoke these words: 390
"The East-Danes' prince, my excellent lord,
bade me say he knows your ancestry,
and you, brave and worthy, are welcome
to him hither across the heaving sea.
Now you may enter in your armor   395
and with helmets on to see Hrothgar;
let your war-shields and deadly wooden spears
await here the outcome of your words."

    The mighty man arose, surrounded   *Beowulf Addresses*
by his stalwart thanes; a few stayed there   *Hrothgar*
to guard their weapons, as he ordered.
The herald guiding, the rest hastened
under Heorot's roof. The hero went,
helmeted, till he stood on the hearth;
Beowulf spoke—his mail-shirt brightly shone,   405
his corselet linked by the smith's skilled craft:
"Great Hrothgar, greetings! I am Hyglac's
kin, he my king. Though young, I've earned much
hard-won glory. Account of Grendel
reached me openly in my own land: 410
sea-men make known that this noble hall
stands empty, useless to anyone,
its brightness dimmed when the light of day

27. West-Danes] See note to l. 1; only a few lines later (391), Wulfgar
calls them *East-Danes*: perhaps the "compass"-epithets suggest the
extensiveness of the Danish kingdom as well as provide the necessary alliteration.

sinks in the evening under the sky.
415   Then the best of my people, those blessed
with courage and wisdom, counseled me,
King Hrothgar, to seek your court and you,
because they'd proved my skill and power:
they themselves saw me come from combat
420   as the victor, where I vanquished five
great giants, rooted out their race; though
sore beset, slew sea-beasts at night,
crushed foes who fiercely sought destruction,
righted the Weders' wrongs; and now I[28]
425   shall face Grendel, that dread foe, alone,
call the bloodthirsty ogre to account.
Bright-Danes' chief, bulwark of the Scyldings,
now I have one favor to request:
that you, protector of the people,
430   not refuse, since I have come so far,
to let me, alone with all my men,
this hardy company, cleanse Heorot.
Further have I heard that the dread foe
in his wild rage scorns using weapons;
435   therefore, that my liege-lord Hyglac may
rejoice in his heart, I too abjure
the use of sword or yellow broad-shield
in battle, but with bare-handed grip
shall I seize the fiend and fight for life,
440   foe against foe; he whom death takes off
must there give himself to God's judgment.
I expect that he will, if he wins
in the battle-hall, feast fearlessly
on Geats, this force of glorious men,
445   as he's fed on Danes. If death takes me,
you will have no need to hide my head

28. Weders] See note to l. 298.

in burial; but he will have me bloody,
will cart off and taste my gory corpse,
solitary will eat me and not mourn,
will mark the moors with blood: you'll need mind   450
no further about my body's fare.
But if battle takes me, send Hyglac back
this rich war-garment which guards my breast,
this corselet that was Hrethel's legacy,
Weland's work. Fate must go as it will!"[29]   455

      Hrothgar, the Scyldings' guardian, spoke: *Hrothgar*   VII
"Beowulf, dear friend, to defend us and   *Welcomes Beowulf*
for honor's sake you have sought us out.
Your father started a deadly feud:
he slew Heatholaf by his own hand   460
among the Wylfings; then the Weders,
fearing combat, could not keep him there.
Thence across the welling of the waves
he sought the South-Danes, the Honor-Scyldings,
when I first ruled the race of the Danes   465
and, though young, reigned over a broad realm,
the citadel of hoard and hero;
for my elder brother—better than I—
Heorogar, Halfdane's son, was dead.
Shortly I settled your father's feud: 470
across the sea I sent the Wylfings
ancient treasures; he swore oaths to me.[30]
My heart sinks with sorrow when I say
to anyone what great injuries,
ghastly crimes, Grendel has committed   475
hatefully in Heorot. My hall-troop,
my warrior host, has shrunk, swept away
by Fate in Grendel's clutch: God easily

29. Weland's work] Any fine piece of armor might be called this, attributing it to Weland, the famous smith of Germanic legend.
30. he] I.e., Ecgtheow, Beowulf's father.

can end the deeds of that mad demon!
480 Frequently, made bold by beer, challengers
have over ale-cups sworn solemn oaths
that they would resist Grendel's onslaught
with their blades' terror in the beer-hall.
Then, when morning dawned, this mead-hall dripped
485 with blood, this royal building was stained
with gore, the bench-planks smeared gruesomely,
a noble hall defiled! I had fewer
dear and loyal warriors: death took them off.
Sit now at the feast, feel free to hear[31]
490 or tell tales of glory, as you choose."

Then a bench was cleared in the beer-hall
for the Geatish troop all together;
there the stouthearted men, proud and strong,
went to sit. A servant with ale-cup
495 richly adorned did his duty, poured
the shining drink. At times the scop sang
clear-voiced in Heort. The heroes, no small
regiment of Danes and Geats, rejoiced.

VIII   *Unferth's Taunt*   Then Unferth, son of Ecglaf, who sat
and Beowulf's Reply   at the feet of the Scyldings' lord, spoke
and stirred up strife; the bold seafarer
Beowulf's venture made him envious,
for he would not grant that anyone
on earth could ever gain more glory
505 under the heavens than he himself:
"Are you that Beowulf who with Breca
strove in swimming on the open sea,
when you two for pride tested the tide
and for a rash boast risked both your lives
510 in deep waters? No one, neither friend
nor foe, could prevent that sad venture

---

31. The meaning of ll. 489–90 has been disputed.

once you two set out upon the sea.
There you embraced the salt sea's billows,
measured with your hands the mainstream's way,
glided over the sea surging high   515
with wintry waves. In the water's hold
you toiled seven nights: he outswam you,
had more strength. In the morning the sea
carried him to the Heatho-Rams' coast;
thence he sought his own dear home, the land   520
of the Brondings, where he was beloved,
a stronghold where he had folk,
fortress, and treasure. Truly the son
of Beanstan fulfilled his boast to you.
Thus I fear you'll find this outcome worse,   525
even though previously you've prevailed
in fierce deeds of battle, if you dare
wait nearby for Grendel all night long."
    Beowulf, Ecgtheow's son, spoke out boldly:
"Indeed, Unferth my friend, drunk with beer   530
you've spoken quite a bit of Breca
and his 'triumph.' Now I'll tell the truth:
I had greater strength at sea, withstood
in the waves more woes than any man.
Being young and rash, as youth is prone   535
to be, we two promised, and then pledged,
that we would venture our very lives
out on the ocean—and so we did.
We held bared swords firmly in our hands
when we two went to sea, thought to defend   540
ourselves from whales. He could not at all
swim away from me over the waves,
speed over waters, nor would I leave him.
So we stayed together in the sea
five nights, till the tide forced us apart: 545
the surging waters, bitter weather,

coal-black night, and a cutting north wind
rounded on us—those waves were rough!
And there the sea-fishes' tempers flared,
550　but my hard, hand-wrought body-armor
stood by me against those hostile ones:
the woven war-garment worked with gold
lay on my breast. One loathsome enemy
dragged me to the depths and held me fast
555　in its fierce grasp; but I was granted
power to pierce that dread foe with the point
of my sword: the battle-storm swept off
that mighty sea-beast through my hand.

　　　"Thus often hostile evil-doers
560　set upon me sorely. I served them
with my good sword such as they deserved:
they had no pleasure in my plenty,
no food from me at their table-feast
in the sea's depths by their evil deeds;
565　but they lay above at the shore's brim
in the morn, sated with my sword-wounds,
put to sleep so soundly by my strokes
they'll take no further toll of travelers
upon the deep. Light dawned from the east,
570　God's bright beacon; the seas subsided,
so that I could at last see headlands,
wind-swept sea-cliffs. So Fate often spares
the undoomed man when his strength endures;
and it happened that I slew with my sword
575　nine sea-monsters by night. I've not heard
of harder fight under heaven's vault,
or a man more savaged in the sea.
But I survived my vile foes' clutches,
tired by my trials. The tidal current,
580　coursing waters, carried me then far
to Lapland. I've not learned of any

IX

such contests of skill or combats like these
on your part. Neither you nor Breca
has yet played in such battle-sport,
performed such a bold and fearless deed   585
with bright swords—not that I boast of it—
although you did slay your own brothers,   kin killing - Unferth
your closest kin; for all your cleverness,
you'll be damned for that, and doomed to hell!
In truth I say to you, Ecglaf's son,   590
that Grendel, that great and dreadful foe,
never would have wrought such wretched harm
in Heort against your lord, if your heart
were so fierce for conflict as you claim;
but he has found he need little fear   595
vengeance from the Victory-Scyldings,
nor dread hail of weapons from this host;
so he takes toll, shows no trace of pity
to the Danes: he does as he pleases,
kills and devours, expects no battle   600
from the Spear-Danes; but respect for the Geats
he'll gain soon, when I bring against him
might and courage. Then whoever can
will go proud to mead when the morning light
dawns next day over the sons of men,   605
and the bright-clothed sun shines from the south."

    Then the giver of treasure, gray-haired   *The Resumption of*
and valiant Hrothgar, was glad at heart: *Festivities*
the Bright-Danes' lord heard Beowulf's resolve,
the people's guardian had hope of help.   610

    There warriors laughed, sounds loudly echoed,
words of cheer went round. Wealhtheow stepped forth;
Hrothgar's good queen, mindful of custom,
gold-adorned, greeted men in the hall.
The courteous lady offered the cup   615
first of all to the East-Danes' ruler,

bade him, beloved of his people, have
joy of that feasting; the famous king
drained the hall-cup, partook heartily.

620 The woman of the Helmings went then
among both tried and young retainers,
proffered precious cups to each of them,
until in time that virtuous queen,
rich with rings, bore the cup to Beowulf;

625 she greeted the warrior Geat, thanked God
with words of wisdom because her wish
was granted: she could count on some man's
aid to end those crimes. He took the cup
from Wealhtheow, and then the warrior, fierce

630 and spoiling for battle, responded—
Beowulf, Ecgtheow's son, spoke out boldly:
"I resolved when I set out to sea,
boarded my boat with my band of men,
that I would gain in full the goodwill

635 of your people, or perish in battle
fast in the demon's grasp. I shall do
a hero's deed, or in this mead-hall
find the end of all my earthly days."
The Geat's brave words, his boasting speech, pleased

640 the lady well; the courteous queen,
gold-adorned, sat down beside her lord.

Preparations for the   Then once again the great hall echoed
Night   with the brave speech of bold conquerors:
the people rejoiced, till presently

645 the son of Halfdane wished to seek
his night's rest: he knew the dreaded foe
determined to attack the high hall
all day long, from the time light first broke
till darkening night deepened over all,

650 and black, shadowy shapes swept forward
under clouds. The company arose.

Then one warrior addressed the other one;
Hrothgar wished Beowulf good luck, control
of the wine-hall, and he spoke these words:
"Never since I could raise hand and shield   655
have I entrusted to any man
save you, now, this noble Danish hall.
Have now and hold the best of houses,
remember glory, make known your might,
watch against the enemy. All gifts   660
are yours if you survive that trial."
　　　Then Hrothgar, defender of the Danes,   X
left the hall with his loyal troop of thanes;
the war-chief wished to seek out Wealhtheow,
his queen-consort. The King of glory,   665
so men heard, had set a special watch
for Grendel in the hall, one to guard
the Danish lord against the demon—
indeed, the bold Geat gladly trusted
in his own great might and in God's grace.   670
Then he removed his iron mail-coat
and his helmet, handed his jeweled sword,
truest of blades, to his attendant,
commanded him to keep his war-gear.
Then the good man, Beowulf of the Geats,   675
made a boast before he sought his bed:
"I put as much faith in my martial
might and power as Grendel puts in his.
Therefore I'll not slay him with a sword,
cut his life off so—although I could.   680
Though noted for fierce deeds, he knows not
our style of fighting, how to strike me,
hew my shield; so this night shall we two
lay sword aside if he dare seek war
without a weapon: let the wise Lord   685
then, holy God, assign the glory

on whichever hand seems fit to Him."
The brave prince then reclined, the pillow
took his head; and his hardy sea-men
690 took their rest around him in the hall.
Not one of them imagined he would
ever seek dear home and hearth again,
see the noble town which nurtured him;
for they knew dark death had previously
695 seized far too many Danish men there
in that wine-hall. But God on high wove
comfort and aid into their fortunes:
and the Weder-Geats gained victory
over their foe by the force and skill
700 of one man's might. Truth is manifest:
Almighty God has always governed
mankind's destiny.

Grendel Visits Heorot   Out of dark night
for the Last Time
swept death's shadow forward. The warders slept,
warriors set to guard that gabled hall—
705 all but one: for men were well aware
that against God's will the evil-doer
could not drag them down into the shadows;
but he in anger watched and waited
for his foe, and for the fight's outcome.

XI   710   Out of the moor then, under mist-hills,
Grendel glided, carrying God's wrath;
the evil monster meant to ensnare
some one of mankind in the high hall.
Under clouds he advanced, till clearly
715 visible the wine-hall rose before him,
shining with gold. Most surely had he
in the past so honored Hrothgar's home;
but he had not found in former days
harder luck or hardier hall-thanes!
720 Up to the door then the demon strode,

joyless, hopeless. It sprang straight open
at his touch for all its fire-forged bands:
enraged, eager to destroy, he wrenched
the hall's mouth wide. Unhesitating,
afire with wrath, the foe stepped upon   725
the shining floor; a wicked gleam shone
from his eyes, a fearful flamelike light.
Inside the hall he saw many men,
a staunch company of young kinsmen,
all asleep; and then his spirit laughed: 730
the dread and fearsome foe, having now
such bounty, meant to draw from body,
before the light of day, each one's life
—and feast! Fate was not so generous:
no more would he feed on human flesh   735
beyond that night. The mighty nephew
of Hyglac observed the sinful beast,
watched how he would try his swift attack;
the dreadful foe delayed no longer,
but in a sudden rush quickly snatched   740
a sleeping warrior, slit him in two,
bit into body, drank blood from veins,
gulped down bite after bite, in no time
consumed the deceased, once-living man,
feet, hands, and all. The foe stepped nearer,   745
reached toward the resolute hero's bed,
laid hands upon him where he lay still,
waiting. Beowulf at once received him
with grim thoughts and leaned against his arm.[32]
Straightway that one steeped in crimes perceived   750

32. leaned against his arm] Some critics take this to mean Beowulf
leaned up on his own arm; others see Beowulf leaning against Grendel's arm and forcing it back in some kind of a wrestling hold. An
analogue often cited in connection with this fight with Grendel is
that of Grettir's fight with Glamr in the Old Icelandic *Grettissaga*.

he had not met in another man
anywhere in the whole wide world
a stronger hand-hold. Fear gripped his heart,
yet there was no way he could escape:
755   he had mind to leave, flee to his lair,
seek fiends' fellowship; for his fare there
differed from that of his former days.
Then Hyglac's valiant kinsman recalled
his evening boasting speech, stood upright
760   and gripped him fast; fingers were bursting,
the ogre moving out, hero advancing.
The infamous one meant, if he might,
to move farther off, flee to the fens;
he could feel his fingers' power crushed
765   by a fierce one's grasp: a grievous trip
for him who had planned harm in Heorot!
The noble hall echoed with the noise
of ale-sharing, but bitter to all[33]
brave Danes who heard it. Both hall-battlers
770   unsheathed their rage. The building shuddered:
it was a wonder that the wine-hall
withstood the fighters, that the fair house
did not fall to earth; but it stood firm,
secured inside and out with iron bands
775   skillfully made. Yet many a mead-bench
studded with gold started from the floor
where the fierce ones fought, as I have heard:
till then knowing Scyldings never thought
that any man could in any way,

33. ale-sharing] Or "ale-deprivation"? A much-discussed crux: I
have taken the passage to suggest the noise made by Beowulf and
Grendel in their struggle is like that in the mead-hall when ale is dispensed, but in the present context ironically bitter to the Danes outside the hall, who hear the noise but do not know how the struggle is
proceeding.

by sheer force or sly cunning, shatter   780
that famed and hornèd hall, unless flames
should swallow it with fire. Frequently
now loud noise arose: for the North-Danes—
hearing that wailing through the wall,
hearing God's adversary howling   785
in defeat, hearing hell's captive chant
a lay of terror, lament his wound—
the sound was fearful. He held him firmly
who was in strength the strongest of men
who lived in that distant day and age.   790

     The champion of warriors did not wish,   XII
by any means, the murderous caller
to leave alive: he held his life's days
little use to men. There his young thanes
swiftly drew and swung their ancient swords: 795
they wished to guard their glorious leader,
save their lord's life if they might do so.
Those brave, noble warriors did not know,
entering the fight with best intentions
to hew and thrust here and there and thus   800
seek Grendel's soul, that no sword on earth,
even the best of iron war-blades,
could make a dent in that miscreant;
for he had worked a spell on weapons
to blunt their edge. And yet his exit   805
from the world, in that day of this life,
was to be dismal, the alien spirit
traveling far into the power of fiends.
Then he who had caused men grief of heart
through many crimes he had committed   810
in feud with God, found to his dismay
that his body would not obey him,
but that Hyglac's fearless kinsman held
his hand fast: each, alive, was hateful

815   to the other. The dread and awesome foe
       suffered sharp distress: on his shoulder
       appeared a vast wound, sinews parted,
       muscles tore from bones. To Beowulf
       glory had been given; and Grendel,
820   death-sick, had to flee down the fen-slopes
       to his joyless lair: he knew full well
       that his life's way, his allotted days,
       had reached an end. After that onslaught
       every Dane had won his heart's desire:
825   the wise and brave warrior from afar
       had cleansed Hrothgar's hall, reclaiming it
       from woe. He rejoiced in that night's work
       of courage and glory: the bold Geat
       had fulfilled his vow to the East-Danes,
830   likewise found a cure for all their care,
       for the great distress they'd undergone,
       for the endless woes they had endured
       in sad necessity. A clear sign
       it was to all, once the brave warrior
835   placed hand, arm, and shoulder, the whole grasp
       of Grendel, under the hall's curved roof.

XIII   Then, as I have heard, to that gift-hall
       many warriors thronged in the morning:
       folk-chieftains journeyed from far and near,
840   from wide-flung parts, to view that wonder,
       the foe's footprints. His parting from life
       brought no woe to any warrior
       who viewed the tracks of that vanquished one,
       who saw how he, dispirited, spent
845   in battle, death-doomed, trailed his life's-blood
       in needy flight to the sea-monsters' mere.[34]
       There the water surged and welled with blood,

34. mere] Lake.

a maelstrom all mingled with hot gore,
streaming and bloodstained as if sword-pierced;
death-doomed he'd hid in his fen-retreat;   850
afterwards, joyless, laid down his life,
his heathen soul: there hell received him.

From that joyous journey old and young   *The Danes Praise*
retainers turned back, riding in high   *Beowulf's Deed*
spirits from the mere, bold men astride   855
gleaming steeds. Beowulf's glorious deed
was there on every tongue: they all said
that no other shield-bearer anywhere,
in the whole wide world from sea to sea
from north to south under the sky's dome,   860
was more deserving of a kingdom—
not that they faulted their friendly lord,
gracious Hrothgar: he was a good king!
At times brave warriors raced bay steeds
in rivalry, giving them their rein   865
where pathways seemed fair and passable
for such contest. At times the king's thane,
a man mindful of many stories,
acquainted with ancient traditions,
wove together fitting words to tell   870
a new tale in true meter; that man[35]
skillfully gave voice to Beowulf's venture,
presenting it appropriately,
varying his words: he revealed all[36]

35. in true meter] A literal translation would be "truly bound"—the
reference is probably to the alliterative binding of verses within the
line (see On the Translation).
36. varying his words] Possibly a reference to the OE technique of
variation (see On the Translation); or possibly it means that the poet
praised Beowulf's deed by comparison to the following story of Sigmund in contrast to that of Heremod—cf. ll. 913–15. At any rate, we
have in ll. 870–74 an example of oral composition, and our only *ars
poetica* for Old English.

875 he'd heard said about Wæls' son Sigmund,[37]
     his valorous deeds and strange events
     that befell him in far wanderings,
     feuds and crimes concealed from everyone
     except for Fitela, his nephew,
880 who was with him, to whom the uncle
     would say all that he wished, since they were
     ever friends in need in every fight
     and together with their swords destroyed
     several giant races. Sigmund gained[38]
885 no little fame when he laid down life
     after he, prince's son, battle-bold,
     killed a dragon guarding gold: under
     a barrow's gray stone he braved the deed
     alone, without the aid of Fitela;
890 but fortune smiled on him: his sword pierced
     the wondrous worm so that the fine steel
     pinned it to the wall; thus it perished.
     By fortitude the fearsome hero
     had earned the jeweled hoard, enjoyed it
895 at his will; so Wæls' son filled a boat,
     bore into the ship's hold shining treasures—
     the worm melted in its mighty heat.

         Of fighting men, Sigmund far surpassed
     others in glory, through great exploits
900 hailed as protector and prospering
     after Heremod's power and might had passed.[39]

37. Lines 875–84—Sigmund] A more specific and somewhat different account of Sigmund's adventures is found in the later Old Norse *Volsungasaga*, chaps. 3–8.
38. Lines 884–97] This account of Sigmund's dragon fight is unique to *Beowulf*. Later Norse and Middle High German accounts attribute such a fight to Sigmund's son Sigurðr / Sigfrit. On the dragon's being consumed by its own heat when killed, cf. l. 3041.
39. Lines 901–15—Heremod] A Danish king of a royal line preceding Scyld and his heirs; it is usually assumed that it was his death that

Heremod, betrayed into his foe's hands
while fighting among giants, forthwith
was dispatched. Too long had surging griefs
lamed and crippled him: to his people,   905
to all princes, he was burdensome.
Many a wise man had often mourned
the ways of that strong-willed warrior,
for they'd trusted him for help for ills,
had hoped that prince's son would prosper,   910
follow in his noble father's steps,
rule well the folk, wealth, and citadel,
the Scyldings' homeland. Hyglac's kinsman
Beowulf was more beloved by all men,
dearer to friends; sin dragged Heremod down.   915

    At times again on the sandy track
they raced their steeds. And morning's light raced
into day. Many a valiant man
hastened then to the high hall to see
that curious wonder; the king himself,   920
the glorious guardian of their treasures,
came from the queen's chamber well attended,
with him the queen and her company
of women went on the mead-hall path. *but assignt lyd destruction with*

    Hrothgar spoke—he had approached the hall,   *Hrothgar's*   XIV
stood on the steps, stared at the high roof   *Gratefulness*
gleaming with gold, and at Grendel's hand:
"For this sight let thanks to Almighty
God be swiftly given! Grief enough
have I endured from Grendel; yet God   930
in His glory works ceaseless wonders.
Not long ago I could not believe

---

left the Danes lordless for a long time, as the beginning of the poem
recounts. Cf. Hrothgar's use of Heremod as a symbol of worldly
pride and mismanagement of the God-given trust of lordship, in ll.
1709–22.

Sarah Higley

I would ever live to see relief
from my woes while this best of houses
stood battle-scarred and stained with blood,   935
a deepening care to my counselors,
who quite despaired of ever saving
our people's fortress from such a foe
as that demonic spirit. Now this man
has, through God's grace and power, done the deed   940
which all of us, for all our powers,
could not perform. Indeed, she who bore
such a son among mankind, if she
still survives, can in all truth say that
Eternal God was gracious to her   945
in childbearing. And now, dear Beowulf,[40]
best of men, in my heart I'll hold you
as a son; keep this new kinship well
evermore. Whatever you desire
of worldly wealth that's mine is now yours.   950
In past times I've paid rewards for less,
spending treasure on less treasured men,
those weaker in war. You yourself have
by your deeds ensured your fame will live
forever. May the Almighty always   955
grant you Godspeed, as He now has done!"
     Beowulf, Ecgtheow's son, spoke out boldly:
"With great goodwill we engaged ourselves
in that bold deed, and daringly braved
the might of the unknown. I wish now   960
you might see the fiend whole before you
in his full gear, weary and fallen:

---

40. Lines 946–49] Whether this is a legal adoption of Beowulf by
Hrothgar has been disputed; but Queen Wealhtheow's reference to
this act in ll. 1175–80, it seems to me, suggests her concern that
Hrothgar may have Beowulf in mind as his successor, instead of his
own sons.

I had hoped to close with him quickly
and bind him upon the bed of death,
965   so that in my sure grip he should gasp
his life out here, and leave his body;
but I could not, when the Lord would not,
keep him from going: I could not cling
firmly enough to my life's foe—he
970   proved too powerful, and fled. He left,
however, his hand, arm, and shoulder
as payment for his life; but little
respite has the wretch gained doing so:
no longer will the evil-doer live
975   with his weight of sins, but his wound will
fetter him close in its forceful grip,
in baleful bonds; there he must abide,
guilt-stained man he is, the great judgment,
how mighty God measures out his doom."

980   Ecglaf's son was a more silent man [41]
in boasting of battle-prowess then,
when, through Beowulf's might, high-born warriors
viewed high on the roof their foe's hand
and fingers: in front of each, in stead
985   of nails, there was the heathen warrior's
spurlike claw, a monstrous spike most like
to steel; each man said no sword, no matter
how well tested that ancient weapon
of fierce men was, could touch the dread foe,
990   harm at all that bloody battle-hand.

XV   *Feasting and*   Then all hands were ordered to adorn
Rewards   Heort within at once. Men and women
soon furbished that festive wine-building,
the Danes' guest-hall. Gold-worked tapestries
995   glittered on the walls, wonderful sights

41. Ecglaf's son] I.e., Unferth.

for all those who like to look on such.
That bright hall, firm-braced with iron bands,
inside had been severely shattered,
its hinges wrenched off; only its roof
had stood steadfast when the dreaded foe,   1000
stained by his foul deeds, turned in his flight
despairing of life. Such an escape
is not easy—let him try who will—
but he must seek that ready place, prepared
for all with souls, for the sons of men   1005
dwelling in this transient world, that place
where his body on its bed of death
sleeps after this life's feast.
                   Then time came
for Halfdane's son to go to his hall:
the king himself wished to grace the feast.   1010
I have not heard a greater host
bear itself better with their treasured lord:
glorious warriors then went to the bench
and feasted well; fairly their kinsmen,
stouthearted Hrothgar and Hrothulf,   1015
accepted many a mead-cup-full
in that high hall. Heorot was, inside,
filled with friends; for then foul treachery[42]
had not shown its face among the Scyldings.
Then Hrothgar gave Beowulf Halfdane's sword,   1020
an ornamented golden ensign,
war-helmet, and corselet as reward;
many saw the famous precious sword
borne in before the warrior. Beowulf[43]

42. Lines 1018–19] Presumably an allusion to later Danish history
when, as other sources suggest, Hrothulf, not Hrothgar's son Hrethric, gained the Danish throne.
43. Lines 1024–25] Evidently by drinking from the cup, Beowulf
acknowledges his acceptance of, and complete satisfaction with,
these rewards.

1025   received the ceremonial cup:
it was no shame to accept such gifts!
I have not heard of many men giving
to another in so friendly fashion
four gold-worked treasures at the feast.

1030   Around the helmet's crown a twisted crest
of wires guarded the wearer from above,
so that no sharp legacy of files,[44]
keen and battle-shower hardened,
in war could shear the shield-warrior's head.

1035   Then the lord of heroes had eight horses
with gold-plated bridles brought inside
onto the floor; on one of them was
a saddle skillfully set with gems;
that was the war-seat of the high king,

1040   when Halfdane's son joined in the sword-play:
never had that prince's prowess failed
when he fought in front where heroes fell.
And then the protector of Ing's friends[45]
bestowed upon Beowulf both horses

1045   and weapons, urged him to use them well.
Thus generously the glorious prince
repaid combat from his precious hoard
of horses and treasures, so that he
who speaks truth could find no fault with them.

XVI   1050   Further, the lord of heroes lavished
treasured heirlooms along the mead-bench
on each man who'd made the sea-voyage
there with Beowulf, and bade gold be paid
for the Geat whom Grendel grievously

1055   had killed—as he'd have killed many more
had not wise God and one man's courage

44. legacy of files] A kenning for "sword"—see On the Translation.
45. Ing's friends] Ing was a legendary Danish king (or god); hence,
his "friends" are the Danes.

forestalled that fate. His Providence ruled
then the race of men, as it rules still.
Therefore foresight, thought for the future,
is always best: he must abide much   1060
of good and evil who lives for long
in these woe-filled days in this dark world.

    There song, together with sweet music,   *Song and Music: the*
swelled before Halfdane's warrior-son;   *Finn Episode*
harp-strings were plucked, and stories retold,   1065
when Hrothgar's scop, for sport in the hall,[46]
entertained the men on the mead-bench:
told how Finn's men fell, and the Scylding[47]
Hnæf, the Half-Danes' hero, in Frisian
slaughter when sudden disaster struck.   1070

    Indeed Hildeburh had little need
to praise the Jutes' good faith: guiltless,
she lost dear ones in the clash of shields,
son and brother, both fated to fall
slain by spear-thrusts—a sad woman, she!   1075
Not without cause could Hoc's daughter mourn
the decree of fate when morning came
and she might see by the bright daylight
her kinsmen killed, where before she'd had

46. scop] The Anglo-Saxon word—or one of them—for "poet."
47. Lines 1068–1159] This so-called Finn Episode is an example
of the stories told as entertainment. Though introduced rather
abruptly, it seems perfectly in keeping with the context, and critics
have seen various parallels between it and the events of the main
story. The beginning of the battle in which Hnæf, Hildeburh's
brother, fell, when the Frisians and Jutes made a sneak attack in early
dawn upon the Half-Danes in their hall while on a visit to King Finn
and Queen Hildeburh, is told in a separate, fragmentary story that
has come down to us, usually referred to as the *Finnsburg Fragment* or
Finnsburh Lay. The Episode in *Beowulf* begins with Hnæf dead,
along with his nephew, Hildeburh and Finn's son. Hnæf's second-in-
command, Hengest, has taken charge of the "woeful few" (ll. 1085,
1099) of the Half-Danes remaining in the hall.

1080 the greatest bliss on earth. Battle had
destroyed all of Finn's thanes but a few,
so that he could not conquer Hengest
face-to-face in the assembly place,
nor expel by force that prince's thane

1085 and his woeful few; so they fashioned terms: [48]
they would clear all of another hall,
floor and dais, which the Danes would share
jointly with the sons of the Jutes;
and Finn, Folkwalda's son, would honor

1090 the Danes each day when gifts were given,
would distribute rings to Hengest's troop,
give them as much of golden treasure
as he chose to cheer his own folk with,
the Frisian host in the drinking hall.

1095 Then they truly pledged a peace-treaty
on both sides: Finn swore most solemnly
to Hengest, in the firmest of oaths,
that as his counselors held, he'd honor
his woeful few, so long as no one

1100 there by words or deeds disturbed the peace,
or plotted cunningly, or complained
though they served the slayer of their lord
being now princeless and compelled by need;
and if any Frisian should provoke

1105 memory of that murderous feud,
then the sword's edge should settle matters.—
A pyre was prepared, and native gold
fetched from Finn's great hoard. Hnæf, the finest

48. Lines 1085–94] The text is ambiguous as to who proposed the
peace terms, the Half-Danes or the Frisians; there is also dispute
about the Jutes: Are they the same as the Frisians, or a tribe allied
with them under Finn's rule? Or does the OE word mean "giants"
and refer to the Frisians under that rubric?

War-Scylding, lay waiting on the pyre.
Easy to see was the bloodstained shirt,   1110
the iron-hard boar-image all-golden,
many a warrior destroyed by wounds:
not a few had fallen in the slaughter!
Then on Hnæf's pyre Hildeburh ordered
her own son placed by his uncle's shoulder,   1115
bones and flesh committed to the flames
to be consumed; sadly the lady
mourned in doleful song as smoke arose:
the mighty death-fire mounted to heaven,
roared before the mound. There heads melted,   1120
and wounds, deadly body-bites, split wide
as the blood sprang forth. Ravenous flame
swallowed all whom war had there destroyed
of both peoples: so their glory passed.

     Then Finn's warriors, bereft of their friends,   1125   XVII
returned to their Frisian fortress towns,
seeking homes and dwellings. But Hengest
spent that winter, slaughter-stained, with Finn,
having no choice: he remembered his home,
but could not steer his ring-prowed ship   1130
upon the sea—the deep welled with storm,
strove with the wind, winter locked the waves
in bonds of ice, till spring burst once more
upon men's dwellings, as it still does,
observing the course of the seasons   1135
with bright weathers. Then winter was past,
earth's bosom fair: the exile fretted,
a guest eager to be gone; yet he thought
more of revenge than riding to sea,
how he could effect an encounter   1140
which would settle his score with the Jutes.
So he did not disdain his duty

when Hunlafing laid the best of swords[49]
which had flamed in battle on his lap:
1145   the Jutes recalled its cutting edges!
So in turn cruel death by the sword came
to stouthearted Finn in his own home,
when Guthlaf and Oslaf spoke their grief,
urged their share of woe and sharp attack
1150   after their voyage: vengeful spirits[50]
could not be restrained. The hall was stained
then with their foes' lives, and Finn, too, slain,
the king with his troop, and the queen taken.
The Scylding warriors bore to their ships
1155   abundance of all jewels and gems
such as they could find there in the home
of the king: they bore across the sea
his noble wife to the Danish nation,
back to her people.

Further Rejoicing and   The poet's tale
Gift-Giving   1160   and song ended. Now joy ascended,
the bench-noise brightened, cup-bearers poured
wine from wondrous vessels. Queen Wealhtheow
then went forth gold-crowned to where that goodly
   pair,[51]

49. Hunlafing] Some critics see this as the name of the sword placed in Hengest's lap, others see it as the name of the son of Hunlaf, brother to the Guthlaf and Oslaf mentioned in l. 1148. In any case, Hengest's acceptance of the sword, whether named or not, indicates his acknowledgment that his duty to revenge his slain lord Hnæf took precedence over his oath of peace to Hnæf's slayer, Finn.
50. The text is not clear as to whether the reference to a voyage is to one made by Guthlaf and Oslaf for reinforcements, or to the original voyage of Hnæf and his men to visit his sister and Finn. The former seems unlikely to me, given the wintry conditions that prevented Hengest from leaving (ll. 1130–33).
51. Lines 1163–68 are hypermetrical in the original; that is, they have three stresses in the first half-line, instead of just two. I have used eleven syllables in these lines, instead of the usual nine (in l. 1166 I admit a twelfth syllable); cf. also ll. 1705–7 and 2995–96.

uncle and nephew, sat; they were still at peace,[52] *allusion to future feud*
each true to the other. And Unferth the thyle   1165
sat at the feet of the Scylding lord: both had faith
in his forthright courage, though to his kinsmen
he'd been less than kind where swords clashed. The
    queen spoke:
    "Accept this cup, kind and noble king,
distributor of treasure! Rejoice,   1170
generous gold-friend to men, and find
gracious words for the Geats, as one should do.
Be magnanimous to them, mindful
of gifts you've gathered from far and near.
I hear that you would have this warrior   1175
for a son. Heorot, this bright ring-hall,
is now cleansed: use freely while you can
many kinds of gifts, but this kingdom
and its people, pass to your own sons
when you depart. For my part, I know   1180
my gracious Hrothulf will guard the youths
honorably should you, Scyldings' friend and lord,
forsake the world sooner than he;
I expect he will repay our sons
in good measure, if he remembers   1185
what kindness we showed him as a child,
furthering his honor and fond hopes."
She went to the bench where her sons were,
Hrethric and Hrothmund, and heroes' sons,
a young warrior band. There the brave man,   1190
Beowulf the Geat, sat by the two brothers.

52. Lines 1164–65] Another allusion to future treachery among the
Danes; see the note to ll. 1018–19. Critics have disagreed about Unferth's role in the treachery. Exactly what court position or function
the OE word *þyle*, which I have kept as "thyle," designated (see also
l. 1456) is much disputed. Opinions range from "court jester" to
"scurrilous fool" to "orator" to "official spokesman"; and Unferth's
character has accordingly been interpreted variously.

XVIII

A cup was carried to him, cordial
words and goodwill offered, twisted gold
graciously bestowed, two great arm-bands,
1195   a shirt of mail, and rings: the neck-ring
the most splendid I've heard spoken of—
none finer, beneath the far-flung skies,
of heroes' treasures, since Hama took[53]
the Brosings' necklace to the bright city,
1200   fled the treacherous feuds of Ermanric
with gem and chain, choosing eternal gain.
(Hyglac the Geat, grandson of Swerting,[54]
wore that neck-ring on his final raid,
when he tried to defend his fortunes,
1205   war-spoils, beneath his flag. Fate claimed him
when, proud with courage, he courted woe,
seeking feud with the Frisians. The prince
wore the gem across the cup of waves:
overseas he fell, under his shield.
1210   Then the king's body, his breast-armor,
and the precious neck-ring passed to the Franks:
weaker warriors despoiled the dead
after the carnage; the Geats' corpses
strewed the field.)

53. Lines 1198–1201] The closest parallel to "the Brosings' necklace"
is the Old Norse *Brisinga men*, a necklace worn by the goddess Freyja
and stolen from her by the god Loki. In the thirteenth-century Old
Norse *Thidrekssaga*, Heimir (OE Hama) is forced to flee from Er-
minrekr (Ermanric), entering a monastery and giving the monks his
armor, weapons, and other treasures; but there is no mention of a
necklace. Perhaps "the bright city" refers to the monastery of the
saga. "Choosing eternal gain" probably refers to Hama's giving up
worldly goods, but it could also be a periphrasis for "died"—cf. l.
2469, where "chose God's light" clearly means the latter.
54. Lines 1202–14] Cf. later accounts of Hyglac's fatal raid, in ll.
2354–59, 2501–8, and 2913–21. In ll. 2172–74, we are told that
Beowulf gave the neck-ring to Hygd, Hyglac's queen; presumably
she in turn gave it to her husband.

Applause surged through the hall.
Wealhtheow spoke, standing before the throng: 1215
"Dear Beowulf, beloved youth, long enjoy
and use well this neck-ring and war-dress
from our people's treasury; prosper,
be bold in your strength, kind of counsel
to these youths: I shall reward you well.   1220
You have performed so men near and far
shall ever praise you and spread your fame
as wide as the sea, home of the winds,
sweeps to distant shores. May destiny
bless you, prince, while you live. I wish you   1225
well of your gifts. In your wealth of joy,
speed my young sons by your splendid deeds!
Here each warrior is true to the other,
peaceable and loyal to his lord;
thanes are as one, the people goodwilled;   1230
warriors well-wined will do as I bid."

meaning: don't double-cross us, or else!

        She sat down. The finest feast was set,
and warriors drank wine. They did not worry
about the grim fate that had befallen
their many comrades after dark came   1235
and mighty Hrothgar had sought his rest
in chamber. Many men occupied
the hall, as they had time and again:
they cleared the bench-planks, spread the floor
with beds and bolsters.—One beer-drinker   1240
took his rest ripe for death, doomed to die.—

foreshadowing

At their heads they set bright battle-shields,
sheltering boards; and there on the bench
above each warrior was visible
his high war-helmet, great wooden spear,   1245
and ringed corselet. It was their custom
to be prepared for war at all hours,
at home or abroad, for whichever

occasion their liege-lord might need
1250   their service: that was a stalwart band.

XIX   *Grendel's*   Then they sank to sleep. One sorely paid
Mother Seeks Revenge   for his evening's rest, as others had
                         when Grendel occupied the gold-hall,
                         committing crimes till his last day came,
1255   death for all his sins: it was clear
       and visible that an avenger
       still survived after that hostile foe,
       after that grievous strife. Grendel's dam,
       a monstrous woman, knew misery,
1260   she who dwelt in the dreaded waters,
       cold currents, after Cain slew with sword
       his only brother, his own father's son:
       he departed then, an exile marked
       with murder, fleeing the joys of men
1265   to wander in the wastelands. From him
       sprang many ghastly demons: Grendel
       was one such hateful fiend, who at Heort
       found a wakeful man awaiting battle;
       there the fearsome foe reached out for him,
1270   but he called upon his strength and skill,
       the copious gift given him by God,
       counted on the Almighty's grace, aid
       and comfort; thus overcame the foe,
       subdued the demon, mankind's enemy,
1275   who then, deprived of joy, departed
       to his death-cell dying. And then still
       his fierce and gloomy mother pursued
       a sorry journey to avenge her son.
              She soon reached Heort where all the Ring-Danes,
1280   heedless, slept throughout the hall. At once
       men's fortunes turned when Grendel's mother
       trod within, though there was less terror
       by as much as women's might and skill

in war compares with armed men's prowess
when the blade forged by the hammer's blows, 1285
the sharp-edged sword shining and bloody,
shears the oncoming helmet's boar-crest.
Then in the hall was the hard-edged sword
snatched from the bench, many a broad shield
raised fast in hand; none thought of helmet 1290
or mail-shirt when the horror seized him.
The monster hastened, wished to quit the hall
to save her life when she was perceived;
swiftly she swooped up a noble thane,
clutched him firmly when she sought the fens: 1295
of all retainers between the seas,
the thane she slaughtered while he slept
was Hrothgar's dearest, a hero famed
for bravery.—Beowulf was not there,
for earlier, after treasure-giving, 1300
the glorious Geat had been lodged elsewhere.—
Heort was in uproar: the hand seized, too,
the well-known bloody arm; sorrow welled
again in every breast. No bargain
was it for either folk, forfeiting 1305
the lives of friends!
          Then the famous king,   *Hrothgar Mourns for*
old and hoary, became sick at heart   *Ashere; the Haunted*
when he learned his thane no longer lived,   *Mere*
knew his dearest, closest comrade dead.
Quickly Beowulf, blessed with victory, 1310
was summoned to the chamber. The champion
went with his warrior band as day broke,
to where the king, with his news of woe,
waited to see if mighty God would
ever change the course of his affairs. 1315
The hero went with his hand-picked troop
across the hall-floor—the timbers creaked—

until he could address directly
the wise lord of Ing's friends, asked him if[55]
1320 he had spent the welcome night he'd wished.

XX   Hrothgar, the Scyldings' guardian, spoke:
"Ask not of joy! Sorrow is renewed
among the Danes. Dead is Ashere,
the elder brother of Yrmenlaf,
1325 who shared my close thoughts and counseled me,
who stood by me shoulder-to-shoulder,
defending our heads when foot-troops clashed,
slashing at boar-crests. Such should men be,
worthy at all times as Ashere was!
1330 A baleful demon became his bane
in Heorot. I do not know whether[56]
the monstrous carrion-eater made off
with full feast; but she avenged the feud
in which last night you ended Grendel's life
1335 violently with your vicelike grip
because he had pursued my people
too long with destruction. He owed a life,
fell in combat; now another's come,
strong and vile, to avenge her kinsman,
1340 and has advanced the feud still further,
as it may seem to many a thane
who grieves with his treasure-giver's[57]

55. Ing's friends] See note to l. 1043.
56. Lines 1331–33] The text is corrupt here; editors and other translators usually emend and suggest something like "I do not know
where the monster went . . . *gladdened* by its feast" (or, ". . . *made
famous by* such slaughter"); but since Hrothgar, only a few lines later
(1357–76) vividly describes the mere where the demons live, I have
kept the MS "hwæþer" (whether) and translated accordingly.
57. My translation of ll. 1342–44 adopts my argument (put forth
elsewhere) that the "treasure-giver" and "powerless hand" refer
to Hrothgar; others take this passage as referring to Ashere as a
treasure-giver in his own right, whose hand now lies lifeless and for

heart's distress; now the hand lies powerless
which helped you to all your hearts' desires.
    "I have heard countrymen and counselors 1345
in my hall and people elsewhere say
they've seen two such alien spirits
haunting the waste borderlands, two huge
monsters holding the moors. One of them,
as best they could perceive, appeared in 1350
woman's shape; the other woeful wretch
measured the exile-paths in man's form,
but larger than any other man.
In olden days dwellers in this land
named him Grendel; they know no father 1355
for him, whether dark, haunting spirits
came before. They live in land unknown,
on wolf-haunted hills, windy headlands,
perilous fen-paths where the mountain stream
plunges down into the headlands' mists, 1360
flows beneath the earth. It is not far
from here in miles to where the mere stands;
frost-bound groves, woods firmly rooted, lean
over it, shadowing its waters.
There one can see a fearful wonder 1365
every night: fire on the flood. No man
breathes so wise as to know its bottom.
Though the heath-stalker, the full-horned hart,
put to flight and far pursued by hounds,
may seek the woods, sooner will he yield 1370
his life up on the shore than leap in
to save his head—hardly a pleasant place!
When the wind stirs up angry storms,

---

whom many a thane grieves in his own distress. Part of my argument is based upon Beowulf's speech in ll. 1384–96.

dark surging waves rise from its surface
1375 to the clouds, till the air grows gloomy
and the heavens weep.
                              Now once again
you are all our hope. You yet know not
that fearful region where you can find
the sinning creature: seek it if you dare!
1380 With wealth I will once more repay you,
with ancient treasures of twisted gold
reward the fight, if you get away."

XXI   *Beowulf
Promises Revenge;
Journey to the Mere*

        Beowulf, Ecgtheow's son, spoke out boldly:
"Grieve not, wise warrior. It is better
to avenge one's friend than mourn too much.
Each of us must one day reach the end
of worldly life; let him who can win
glory before he dies: that lives on
after him, when he lifeless lies.
1390 Rise, kingdom's guardian; quickly let us
go and view the track of Grendel's kin.
I promise you she will not escape:[58]
nor in earth's womb, nor in mountain wood,
nor in seas' far depths, flee where she will!
1395 For this day be patient and endure
every woe, as I believe you will."
        The old king leapt up, gave thanks to God,
the mighty Lord, for the man's good speech.
Then men bridled a horse for Hrothgar,
1400 a steed with braided mane: the wise prince
rode splendidly arrayed. Shield-bearers
marched along on foot. The forest-paths,
the trail along the ground, were marked with tracks
easy to see, as she had moved straight

58. Lines 1392, 1394—she] The MS uses the pronoun *he*—the sex of
Grendel's mother is confused on several occasions.

Sarah Higley

1405   across the murky moor carrying
        lifeless the body of the best thane
        who helped Hrothgar keep watch at home.
        The king and his noble company
        climbed steep rock-slopes, followed narrow paths
1410   single file, an unfamiliar course
        over high headlands by sea-beasts' lairs.
        He, with a few of his counselors,
        rode ahead to scout the strange terrain,
        till suddenly he saw mountain trees
1415   leaning out over a large gray rock—
        a cheerless wood; below, water stood
        churning and gory. There was anguish
        in the heart of every Dane, of each
        friend of the Scyldings, sharp pain and grief
1420   for each thane, when by the water there,
        on the high cliff, they found Ashere's head.
        The flood spouted blood, steamed with hot gore—
        the men stared. At times a horn sang out
        an eager war-call. The troop all sat down:
1425   they saw, then, swimming in the water
        many serpents and strange sea-dragons,
        and on the cliff-slopes others sleeping,
        such serpents and wild beasts as often
        on dark morns make journeys sorrowful
1430   for those who sail the sea. The monsters fled,
        bitter and enraged: they heard the horn's
        bright battle cry. A Geatish bowman[59]
        relieved one of them of life and wave-
        contending: his hard arrow bit deep
1435   into its heart, slowing its swimming
        in the water as death took it away.
        It was quickly assailed in the waves

59. Some take the Geatish bowman as Beowulf himself.

with boar-spears sharply barbed, forcefully
dragged to shore and drawn up on the cliff:
a wondrous wave-roamer; the warriors   1440
stared at their dreadful guest.
                          Beowulf dressed   *Beowulf Arms Himself*
himself in armor, felt no fear at all: *to Fight Grendel's*
his corselet, broad and cunningly worked,   *Mother*
handwoven, had to sound the water;
it knew how to hold the body safe   1445
so no foe's grasp, no furious assault,
could touch his heart, take away his life;
and the bright helmet guarded his head—
it would soon seek the surging waters,
plunge with its splendid ornaments down   1450
to the mere-floor's mud: in former days
a smith had made and subtly shaped it,
studded it with boar-figures so that
sword or blade never could bite through it.
Not the least of mighty aids was lent   1455
to him in his need by Hrothgar's thyle,[60]
the long-hilted sword called Hrunting,
outstanding among ancient treasures:
its iron blade, bright with serpentine
design and hard with blood of battle,   1460
had failed none who'd dared grasp it in hand
and go forth into perilous fight
on the field of foes; for not the first time
should it perform a feat of courage.
Indeed Ecglaf's son, strong and skillful,[61]   1465
did not recall what he had spoken
drunk with wine, when he lent that weapon
to the better swordsman; he himself
dared not risk his life in valorous deed

60. Hrothgar's thyle] I.e., Unferth, on *thyle*, see note to ll. 1164–65.
61. Ecglaf's son] I.e., Unferth.

XXII

1470 beneath the lashing waves; there he lost
fame for bravery. Not so Beowulf,
once he had dressed himself for battle.
        Beowulf, Ecgtheow's son, spoke out boldly:
"O famous son of Halfdane, wise king,
1475 remember, now that I am ready
for this venture, what we said before:
if at your great need, gold-friend of men,
I should not return, you still would take
a father's place to my departed soul.
1480 Be refuge to my young retainers,
my hand-picked warriors, if war takes me,
and those treasures which you tendered me,
belovèd Hrothgar, send to Hyglac.
When the Geats' lord, Hrethel's son, perceives
1485 that gold munificence, he will know
I found here a ring-giver fully
generous, enjoyed him while I could.
And let Unferth, famous far and wide,
have this wondrous heirloom, wave-patterned
1490 and sharp-edged sword; with Hrunting shall I
carve out fame, or death will vanquish me."

The Fight with
Grendel's Mother

        After these words the Weder-Geat turned
boldly away—he would not await
an answer: the surging water swallowed
1495 the warrior. Then it was a good while
before he could perceive the sea-floor.
At once she who had dwelt war-eager,
fierce and greedy for fifty years
in the sea's domain, saw that some man
1500 explored from above her alien lair.
She grasped at him, and grabbed the warrior
with horrible claws, yet could not harm him;
his body was unscathed: his armor
ringed it round so that she could not thrust

loathsome fingers through the linked mail-coat.   1505
When the sea wolf reached bottom, she bore
the ring-saved hero to her lair, bore
him so he could not, brave as he was,
use weapon; many wondrous beings
harassed him in the water, assailed   1510
his mail-shirt with tusks: monstrous sea-beasts
pursued him. Then the warrior perceived
that he was inside a hostile hall
where water could not harm him at all,
nor tide's sudden surge touch and seize him,   1515
because of the roof. He saw firelight
with a whitish flame flaring brightly.
    Then the brave man could see the barbarous
mere-hag; he swung his sword mightily—
his hand did not stay the stroke—so that   1520
the wave-patterned blade sang a war-song
fiercely on her head. Then her guest found
that the flashing war-blade would not bite
and harm her life: its edge failed the prince
in his need; before, it had endured   1525
many hand-combats, shearing helmets
and doomed men's war-dress; so it was then
first that the rare treasure's glory failed.
    Hyglac's kinsman, not slow in courage,
mindful of fame, nonetheless stood firm: 1530
the angry warrior cast the coil-patterned,
decorated sword down to the ground,
tough and steel-edged; he trusted his strength,
his hand-grip's force. Thus must one perform
when he hopes to win long-lasting praise   1535
in combat: never care about his life!
So the War-Geat did not fear the fight:
he seized Grendel's dam by the shoulder;
battle-bold and furious, he flung

1540 his life's foe so she fell to the floor.
Quickly she handed him a like gift
in turn, clutching him in her sharp claws;
the strongest of foot-fighters stumbled
with weariness then, and down he went.
1545 She then straddled her hall-guest and drew
her wide, bright knife; she wished to avenge
her son and only heir. The meshed armor
across his shoulder sheltered his life,
preventing entry of point and edge;
1550 Ecgtheow's son would indeed have perished
under the broad earth if that battle-coat
with its hard woven mesh had not helped
the Geatish champion—and Holy God
brought victory in war; the wise Lord,
1555 Heaven's Ruler, rightly decided it
easily, once Beowulf stood up again.

XXIII   Then he saw there among other arms
an invincible and strong-edged blade—
a joy to warriors, made by giants
1560 long ago: excellent, but larger
than any other man might bear to
war-play, this splendid work of giants.
Savage and fierce, the Danes' defender
seized the linked hilt; despairing of life,
1565 drew the ring-adorned sword; in wrath struck
so that it hit her hard on the neck
and broke her bone-rings; the blade cut through
the doomed flesh: down she fell to the floor.
The sword was bloody; Beowulf rejoiced.
1570   The light blazed, the glow within brightened,
just as from the sky Heaven's candle
shines clear. He glanced throughout the chamber,
then moved by the wall, raised the weapon
firmly by its hilt; to Hyglac's thane,

the wrathful and resolute warrior,   1575
its edge was not useless: for he would
now repay Grendel all those ghastly
attacks he had wrought on the West-Danes,
starting with that first time long ago
when he slew Hrothgar's hearth-companions   1580
in their sleep, devoured on the spot
fifteen men of the Danish nation,
and carried off an equal number,
a hideous booty. The fierce hero
had requited him for that: he saw   1585
Grendel at rest, greatly wearied by war,
lifeless, just as battle had leeched him
in Heort. Now his body burst open,
suffering a sword-stroke after his death,
a hard blow: Beowulf cut off his head   1590
    At once Hrothgar's wise men, those watching
the waters, saw the surging waves
were all stirred up, that the mere was stained
with blood. The gray-bearded elders spoke
together about the good warrior,   1595
said they did not think that noble one
would return victorious to seek
their glorious king: to a good many
it seemed the sea wolf had destroyed him.
Came the ninth hour: the courageous Danes[62]   1600
left the slope, and likewise their gold-friend
set out homeward. Their Geatish guests sat
sick in spirit and stared at the mere;
they wished, but did not expect, to see
their dear lord himself.   1605
                Below, the sword
began to shrink: the war-blade shriveled
into bloody battle-icicles;

62. ninth hour] I.e., 3 P.M.

wondrously it melted, most like ice
when the Father releases frost's bonds,
1610   unbinds the tied stream, He who controls
times and seasons: that is the true Lord.
The Weder-Geat took no more treasures
from the site, though he saw many there,
than the head together with the hilt
1615   bright with jewels; the wave-patterned blade
had burnt up in the poisonous hot blood
of the demon who had died within.
At once the victor entered the water,
dove up, left his fallen foes behind.
1620   The surging waves, great tracts of water,
were all cleansed, now the alien spirit
had forfeited life and this fleeting world.

The Hero's Return to   Then the stouthearted sea-men's leader
Heorot   swam to shore, rejoicing in sea-booty,
1625   in the great burden he brought with him.
His splendid troop of thanes went towards him,
thanking God and rejoicing that they
could again see their prince safe and sound.
Then helmet and corselet were quickly
1630   removed from the hero. The mere drowsed
beneath the skies, still stained with blood.
They went forth thence, retracing their steps
happy in their hearts, pacing the path
and well-known road; brave kingly warriors
1635   carried the head away from the cliff,
a hard task for each great-hearted one
by himself: four of them had to bear
Grendel's head, with great difficulty,
on the shaft of a spear to the gold-hall,
1640   until finally the fourteen Geats,
bold and courageous, came to the hall;
among them their lord, proud in that throng,

pressed across the surrounding plain.
Then the thanes' leader, brave in battle
and made famous by his fearless deeds,   1645
entered the mead-hall to greet Hrothgar.
And Grendel's head was borne by the hair
across the floor where men were drinking—
a ghastly sight for them and their queen;
the men stared at the strange spectacle.   1650

    Beowulf, Ecgtheow's son, spoke out boldly: XXIV
"Behold, son of Halfdane, great Scylding,
gladly we've brought you this sea-booty,
token of success, for you to see.
Not lightly did I escape with life   1655
from that underwater fight; I dared
the deed at great risk: my fighting days
soon had ceased had God not shielded me.
In battle Hrunting could not help me,
as excellent as that weapon is;   1660
but the Ruler of men granted me
that I should see a huge ancient sword
hanging fair on the wall—how often
He guides the friendless!—and I drew it;
in course of battle killed the guardians   1665
of that place. Then the wave-patterned blade
burnt up as blood burst forth, the hottest
shed in combat. I carried the hilt
away: I avenged those wicked deeds,
killings of Danes, as was right to do.   1670
This I promise you: that you may sleep
in Heort free from care with all your host,
retainers young and old, every thane
among your nation; you need not fear
death for your warriors, lord of the Danes,   1675
from that direction, as you did before."
    Then the golden hilt, the age-old work

of giants, was handed to Hrothgar,
the old chief; with the fall of the fiends,
1680   the well-wrought piece passed into control
of the Danish prince: when the demon,
foe to God and man, guilty of murder,
turned from this world—and his mother, too—
it passed into the power of the best
1685   of worldly kings between the seas
who shared their wealth in the Danish realm.

Hrothgar's Sermon and   Hrothgar spoke, viewing the heirloom hilt,
Advice to Beowulf   on which the origin of ancient
strife was written: rushing flood waters[63]
1690   afterwards destroyed the race of giants—
alien to Eternal God, they did
terrible things: the Ruler gave them
reward for that through the waters' surge.
On the sword-guards of bright gold, rightly[64]
1695   marked out by rune-staves, it was thus set
down and told for whom that best of swords,
with twisted hilt and serpentine design,
had first been made. All fell silent then,
as the wise son of Halfdane spoke:
1700   "Lo, he who acts with truth and justice,
long guarding folk and land, recalling
all far past, can say this warrior was
born the finer man! Now fame extends
itself far and wide, Beowulf my friend,
1705   —yours among all nations. With mind's wisdom you[65]
steadily control your strength. I shall keep my pledge,
as we spoke before. You will be a comfort

63. Lines 1689–93] An allusion to the biblical flood; cf. note to l. 114.
64. Lines 1694–98—rune-staves] Inscription of this sort on metal, stone, or horn was done in the runic alphabet of the ancient Germanic peoples.
65. Lines 1705–7 are hypermetric; see note to ll. 1163–68.

all long-enduring to your people,
a help to men. Not so was Heremod[66]
to Ecgwela's sons, the Honor-Scyldings;   1710
he grew up not as joy but as death
and destruction to the Danish race:
enraged, he killed his feasting-comrades,
loyal warriors, till that well-known prince,
exiled, alone, left the joys of men.   1715
Though God Almighty had granted him
above all men delight in great might
and power, yet his heart grew perverse,
greedy for blood: he gave no rings
to the Danes to gain glory; joyless   1720
he dwelt, suffering distress from this strife,
his people's lasting hate. Learn by this,
know man's true virtue. An aging man,
I've told this tale for you.
                          Wondrous to tell
how mighty God distributes to men,   1725
through His great goodness, wisdom and land
and noble rank: He has rule of all!
At times He lets a man of high lineage
have all his mind and heart desire:
gives him earthly bliss in his homeland,   1730
a stronghold of men to control,
dominion over many worldly parts,
a broad kingdom—so that he cannot
in his folly imagine its fall.
He lives in luxury, knows nothing   1735
of illness or old age; nor does dread
care darken his heart, nor hatred bare
sword anywhere; but the whole world turns

66. Lines 1709–22] See note to ll. 901–15; Ecgwela] an otherwise unknown Danish king.

at his own will: he knows nothing worse—

XXV   1740   till his portion of pride grows and puffs
up inside him; then the watchman sleeps:
the soul's keeper, engrossed in worldly cares,
sleeps too soundly, the slayer too near[67]
who shoots from his bow with baleful aim.

1745   Then under his guard his heart is hit
with sharp-filed arrows he cannot fend,
with the devil's dark crooked promptings;
what he's held long seems all too little:
greedy he hoards, without honor gives

1750   no golden rings, forgets and neglects
what is to come, because God, Heaven's King,
earlier gave him so much glory.
In time it happens in his turn
that his fleeting and fated body

1755   totters and falls; someone else takes all,
painlessly, without compunction,
shares widely that noble's ancient wealth.
    "Keep yourself, dear Beowulf, best of men,
from that baleful path; choose the better:

1760   eternal gains. Avoid all pride,
illustrious man. But a little while
will your power bloom; soon it will be
that sickness or sword will strip your strength,
or the fire's grip, or the flood's great surge,

1765   or the sword's thrust, or the spear's swift flight,
or terrible old age; or your eyes'
clear light will cloud and dim: all at once,
warrior, death will overpower you.
    "Thus I ruled the Ring-Danes fifty years

1770   beneath these skies, shielded them in war
from many nations in the known world

67. Lines 1743–44] Some have seen here an echo of the biblical image of the devil's arrows and spiritual armor in Ephesians 6:13–17.

with spears and swords, so that I feared no
adversary under the heavens.
Alas, a change came in my own land,
grief after joy, when Grendel, ancient   1775
adversary, was my invader:
I ever suffered sad heart's distress
for that affliction. Thanks be to God,
the Eternal Lord, that I have lived
to see with my own eyes, after all   1780
that strife, the bloodstained, gory head!
Now take your seat: victorious, share
in our happy feast; we two shall share
many fine treasures when morning comes."

  The Geat was glad at heart, and straightway   1785
went and sat down, as the wise king bade.
Then once more, as before, a fair feast
was served to valiant warriors sitting
in the hall.

    Night's shadows settled in,
dark over heroes. That host all rose: 1790
the gray-haired, agèd Scylding wished to
seek his bed; the brave Geat shield-warrior,
weary from his venture, was well pleased
to rest. A chamberlain at once led
forth the traveler from afar, tended   1795
courteously to all the thane's comforts,
those such as in that day sea-warriors
could well expect as their proper due.

  Then the hero rested, the hall towered   *The Geats Depart from*
arched and gold-adorned; the guest slept on   *Denmark*
till the black raven blithely announced
the sun, Heaven's joy; the bright light hastened
departing shadows; warriors made haste,
noblemen eager to journey home
to their people; the proud-spirited   1805

visitor wished to seek his far-off ship.
    Then Ecglaf's bold son had Hrunting brought[68]
to Beowulf, and bade him take the sword,
the precious blade; Beowulf praised the gift,
1810   thanked him and said he thought it a friend
in battle, war-worthy; spoke no blame
against its edge: a gallant spirit!
Then the warriors, equipped in armor,
were eager to leave; their princely leader,
1815   dear to the Danes, walked to the dais
where Hrothgar sat, and greeted him.

XXVI   Beowulf, Ecgtheow's son, spoke out boldly:
"Now we seafarers come from afar
wish to say that we long to seek
1820   Hyglac. We have been treated well here,
entertained as well as we could wish.
If in any way by warlike deeds
on earth I might earn more of your heart's
affection than I have done before,
1825   lord of warriors, I shall come at once.
If I hear across the coursing sea
that neighboring tribes terribly threaten you,
as your enemies at times have done,
I'll bring a thousand thanes, brave heroes,
1830   to your aid. As for Hyglac, I know
that the Geat's lord and nation's guardian,
young though he may be, will give me help
by words and deeds to honor my word;
I'll bring a forest of spears, support

68. Lines 1807–9] Although not mentioned in the action, Beowulf had obviously brought Hrunting back with him, along with Grendel's head and the giant sword-hilt, from beneath the mere. Whether Unferth is here making a present of the sword to Beowulf, as I have translated it, or whether Beowulf is now returning the sword to Unferth at his departure, is not clear.

of great might, if you have need of men.   1835
If Hrethric, your princely son, should be pleased
to seek the Geatish court, he can count
there on many friends: far countries are
best sought by one who himself is strong."
     Hrothgar spoke out and gave him answer: 1840
"The wise Lord has sent the words you've said
into your mind: more wisely I've not
heard one speak who is so young in years.
You are strong in might and ripe in mind,
wisdom hangs on your lips! I expect,   1845
should spear or sword take off Hrethel's son
in fierce and bloody battle, or should
dread illness waste away your lord,
the people's guardian, and you yet live,
that the Sea-Geats could not choose a king   1850
better than you to guard their treasure,
if you wish to rule your kinsmen's realm.
The longer I know you, dear Beowulf,
the better your spirit pleases me.
You have brought about mutual peace   1855
between our peoples, the Weder-Geats
and Spear-Danes; and strife and hostile acts
which once they practiced, are put to rest.
While I rule this wide realm, we'll share our
treasures: goodly gifts will one man take   1860
another across the gannet's bath,
the ring-prowed ship bring presents of love
across the sea. I know our countries'
peoples will stand fast toward friend and foe,
act blamelessly, in the ancient way."   1865
     Then the lord of heroes, Halfdane's son,
gave him twelve more treasures in the hall;
bade him go safely with those presents
to his people, speedily return.

1870 The Scylding prince, king nobly descended,
     then kissed the best of thanes and clasped him
     by the neck; tears coursed naked down the cheeks
     of the gray-haired one: wise with his years,
     he knew it unlikely that they two
1875 would ever meet afterward again
     brave in council. Beowulf was so dear,
     he could not restrain his emotion,
     for fast in his breast's firm core, deep-felt
     longing for the belovèd man burned
1880 in his blood. Away from him Beowulf,
     warrior proud with gold, trod the grass-plain,
     exulting in treasure; awaiting
     its owner, the ship rode at anchor.
     On the journey Hrothgar's generousness
1885 was much praised; he was a peerless king,
     faultless in all respects, till old age,
     which ruins many, robbed him of his strength.

XXVII
             Then that troop of brave young retainers
     came to the water, wearing their coats
1890 of interlocked mail. The land-warden marked
     their return, as he had their arrival.
     He did not greet those guests with insults
     from the cliff's ridge, but rode to meet them,
     said the bright-clad warriors shipward bound
1895 would be most welcome to the Weders.
     The spacious ring-prowed ship was loaded
     then on the beach with battle-garments,
     horses, and treasures; its mast towered
     over Hrothgar's hoard of stored-up wealth.
1900 Beowulf gave the boat-guard a sword bound[69]
     with gold, so that afterwards he gained

---

69. boat-guard] Is this the "Scyldings' warden" of ll. 229–30, or one
of the "young thanes" he assigned to guard the Danes' boat (l. 293)?

more honor by that treasured heirloom
on the mead-bench. The ship moved outward
to plow the deep, leaving Danish land.
Then a sea-cloth, a sail, was made fast   1905
by rope to the mast; the sea-planks creaked.
No wind there kept the ship from its way
over the waves: seaworthy, it went forth
with tight-bound and foamy prow, floating
from wave to wave across the currents,   1910
till they caught sight of the Geatish cliffs,
well-known headlands; impelled by the wind,
the keel pressed up and stood on the shore.
The harbor-guard was ready at the shore,
who for long had looked far out to sea   1915
with longing for the belovèd men:
he moored the broad-beamed ship on the beach
fast with anchor-ropes, lest the waves' force
should drive the fair wooden ship away.
Beowulf then bade the wealth of princes,   1920
ornaments and plated gold, brought up;
not far thence dwelt their treasure-giver,
Hyglac, Hrethel's son, who with his thanes
kept his royal seat near the seawall.

    The building was fair, the famous king   1925
set high in the hall, Hygd very young;[70]   — Hyglac's wife, Queen
though Hæreth's daughter had dwelt but few years
within fortress walls, she was still wise
and accomplished: she was not cruel,
nor too sparing to the Geats in gifts   1930
and treasures.
            Modthryth did dreadful things,[71]   *The Modthryth-Offa*
till she became an excellent queen: *Episode*

70. Hygd] Daughter of Hæreth; Hyglac's wife, queen of the Geats.
71. Lines 1931–43] The introduction of the young princess Modthryth (or Thryth?) and her cruel behavior is rather sudden but in

she would not permit any brave man
of her following, unless a great lord,
1935   to dare set eyes on her openly;
if he did, he would find fatal bonds
awaiting him, after which straightway
death by the sword was decreed for him:
the branch-patterned blade would settle it,
1940   proclaiming death. No queenly custom
for a lady, lovely though she be:
Freawebba   that a _peace-weaver_ deprive of life
a dear fine man for such fancied wrong!
Offa, Hemming's kinsman, halted that:[72]
1945   ale-drinkers then told a different tale,
how she performed fewer deadly crimes
against men once she had been given
gold-adorned to the dear young noble
warrior—once she had sought Offa's hall,
1950   following her father's bidding,
across the gray-green sea; thereafter
enthroned, famous for munificence,
she used well her life's allotted days,
deeply loved the leader of heroes
1955   who was, as I have heard, best of all
mankind who occupied the land
between the seas. Offa was widely

---

keeping with the poet's use of juxtaposition to create contrast (in this
case, with the generous behavior of Hygd).
72. Lines 1944–60] Offa was a fourth-century king of the Angles,
whose greatest feat, victory in single combat by the Eider River to
save his kingdom, is alluded to in the OE poem *Widsith*. Here the
poet is concerned more particularly with his "taming of the shrew,"
Modthryth. As to why the poet has included this long digression on
Offa, there has been much speculation: perhaps as a eulogy for his
English descendant, Offa II, the great Mercian king, who ruled in
the last half of the eighth century—this is the only "English" reference in the poem.

honored for gifts given and wars won:
brave with spear abroad, he ruled wisely
in his homeland. From him sprang Eomer   1960
as help for heroes: Hemming's kinsman,
Garmund's grandson, was skilled in combat.

    Then Beowulf trod with his hand-picked troop
along the sea-strand's wide and sandy
shores. Hastening from the south, the sun shone,
candle to the world. They went their way,   1965
striding with great haste to where they heard
their good young war-king, shield of warriors,
Ongentheow's slayer, shared out rings[73]
within the stronghold. Straightway Hyglac   1970
was brought the news of Beowulf's return:
that come there was his comrade-in-arms,
shield of heroes, alive to his home,
sound from battle-play safe to the court.
Room in the hall was quickly arranged   1975
for the foot-guests, as the great king bade.
Then the conquering hero sat, kinsman
opposite kinsman, after the lord
greeted his loyal thane graciously
and formally. Throughout that fair hall   1980
Hæreth's daughter moved with mead-cups, cared
kindly for the people, poured strong drink
into warriors' cups. Hyglac questioned
his companion in the high hall
courteously: curiosity pricked him   1985
as to what success the Sea-Geats had:
"How did your journey fare, dear Beowulf,

*Beowulf
and Hyglac*   XXVIII

---

73. Ongentheow's slayer] Although here King Hyglac is called the
slayer of the Swedish king, we discover that one of his thanes, Eofor
(and his brother Wulf) did the actual slaying—see the account of
Ongentheow's victory over Hyglac's brother Hæthcyn and Hyglac's
subsequent revenge, ll. 2922–88.

when you suddenly resolved to seek
combat and battle across salt seas
1990   in distant Heort? And did you at all
help cure the wide-known woe of Hrothgar,
the famous king? Heart's care I've suffered,
sorrow's surgings, for I had no faith
in your purpose, dear friend; I pleaded
1995   long that you should not confront that fiend,
but let the South-Danes themselves settle
their war with Grendel. I give God thanks
that I may see you here safe and sound."
        Beowulf, Ecgtheow's son, spoke out boldly:
2000   "That great encounter is no secret
to many men, my lord Hyglac—what long
grappling Grendel and I engaged in,
there where he had caused countless sorrows
and made life miserable for all
2005   the Victory-Scyldings; I avenged all that,
so not one of Grendel's worldly kin,
who lives longest of that loathesome race
enmeshed in his sin, will need much boast
of that fight by night. First I came there
2010   and greeted Hrothgar in the ring-hall;
as soon as he knew my mind's intent,
Halfdane's well-known son at once assigned
a seat to me facing his own sons.
The company rejoiced. Never have
2015   I seen under heaven's vault hall-joys
more infectious. At times the famous queen,
the pledge of peace, passed throughout that hall,
urged the young men on; often she gave
one a bracelet before she sat down.

The Ingeld   2020   At times to the tried retainers
Episode   Hrothgar's daughter carried the ale-cups:
                 I heard heroes in the hall call her

Freawaru, as she offered warriors
the studded goblet. Young, gold-adorned,
she is promised to Froda's fair son;[74]   2025
the Scylding king and kingdom's keeper
has resolved this, and thinks the plan good:
that with this woman he can manage
to settle old feuds. But too seldom
after a king's death does deadly spear   2030
rest for long, however right the bride!
     "It may displease the Heatho-beard prince,
and all the thanes of his people,
when he walks in the hall with his wife
and her young Danes are being well dined: 2035
on the Danes will gleam Heatho-beard gold,
hard heirloom swords of their ancestors,[75]
who kept them while they could wield weapons,
     till where shields crashed in combat they led   [XXIX]
their comrades and themselves to costly death.   2040
At the beer-feast an old spear-fighter,
seeing that display, recalling then
with grim spirit the spear-death of men,
with gloomy mind will test the mettle
of a young warrior, waking war-thoughts   2045
through heart's sorrow, saying words like these:

74. Lines 2025–69—Froda's fair son] I.e., Ingeld, who ruled the
Heatho-beards after his father died in the feud with the Danish
Scyldings. In the lines that follow, Beowulf hypothecates the likely
failure of Hrothgar's effort to resolve the feud by marrying his
daughter Freawaru to Ingeld. The story of this feud, and of Ingeld in
particular, was evidently well known in one form or another among
the Germanic peoples, and popular even in English monasteries, as
Alcuin's famous adjuration "Quid Hinieldus cum Christo?" ("What
has Ingeld to do with Christ?"), in his letter of 797 to the monks at
Lindisfarne, attests. The OE poem *Widsith* tells how "Hrothulf and
Hrothgar . . . humbled Ingeld's battle-array, cut down at Heorot the
host of the Heatho-beards."
75. their] I.e., the Heatho-beards'.

'Can you, my friend, recognize that sword,
the precious blade which your father bore
when he wore his masked helmet to war
2050   for the last time, where the Danes slew him
when Withergild and his warriors fell,[76]
and those fierce Scyldings possessed the field?
Now the son of one of those slayers
struts in our hall in all those trappings,
2055   boasts of that slaying and bears the treasure
which you by rights should yourself possess.'
Thus will he urge him, and endlessly
remind with cruel words, till the moment
Freawaru's thane, for his father's deeds,
2060   sleeps bloodstained from the sword's cruel bite,
his life forfeit, while the other flees
alive and safe, knowing the land well.
Then on both sides warriors' oaths will be
broken; soon bitter hate will well up
2065   in Ingeld, and in his great anguish
love for his wife will languish and cool.
Thus I have no faith in Heatho-beard
promises, or sincere peace with the Danes,
or firm friendship.
                                    Yet further let me,

Beowulf Recounts His
Fights with the Grendel   o giver of treasure, speak of Grendel,
Clan   so you may clearly know the outcome
of our hand-fight. Once heaven's jewel
glided over earth, the angry demon,
dread spirit of the night, sought us out
2075   where we, unharmed, watched over the hall.
There his attack doomed Handscio to death,[77]

76. Withergild] Presumably a well-known warrior of the Heatho-
beards.
77. Handscio] The Geatish warrior eaten by Grendel, ll. 740–45,
not previously named.

fatal destruction; he was first to fall,
armed though he was; Grendel ended life
for that belovèd man—with his mouth:
gulped down the good thane's entire body.   2080
Even then the slayer bloody-toothed,
his mind set on evil, had no mind
to leave the gold-hall empty-handed;
but strong in his might made trial of me,
grasped me with eager hand. A glove hung   2085
huge and strange, fastened with cunning straps:
it had been fashioned skillfully
by devil's art from dragon skins.
The rash miscreant wished to stick me
therein, innocent though I was, as   2090
one of many; he might not do so,
though, when I in my wrath stood upright.
    "Too long to tell how for every crime   [XXX]
I handily repaid that people's scourge;
and there, dear prince, my deeds brought honor   2095
to your people. Though he slipped away
and enjoyed life for a little while,
yet his right hand remained in Heorot:
he passed from there wretched and depressed,
and dying fell to the mere's far depths.   2100
For that deadly strife, the Scylding lord
rewarded me with much plated gold,
with many treasures when morning came
and we were all feted at the feast.
There was song and mirth. The old Scylding,[78]   2105

78. Lines 2105–14] The passage is ambiguous. Critics disagree as to
how many storytellers Beowulf is referring to. Perhaps "the old
Scylding" of l. 2105 refers to the "king's thane" of l. 867, and "the
man proved in war" of l. 2107 to the scop who tells the Finn Episode;
and these may be one and the same. The "generous king" of l. 2109
and the "old warrior" of l. 2111 clearly seem both to refer to
Hrothgar.

well informed, spoke much of far-off days;
at times the man proved in war plucked joy
from the harp, sometimes rehearsed a tale
true and sad; at times the generous king
2110 would tell some strange story fittingly;
sometimes the old warrior, bowed with age,
would mourn in turn his lost youth and loss
of strength in war: his heart welled within
when, old and wise, he recollected all.
2115   "Thus there within we took our pleasure
all day long, until another night
came to men. Quickly Grendel's mother,
ready for revenge, journeyed in sorrow,
remembering that death had seized her son
2120 in war with Geats. The monstrous woman
avenged her son, violently killed
a warrior: the wise old counselor
Ashere there had his life extinguished.
Nor, when morning came, could the Danes
2125 commit the beloved man to the flame,
placing him on the funeral pyre:
for she bore off his body in her
fiend's embrace beneath the mountain stream.
For Hrothgar that was the bitterest grief
2130 that might long befall that people's prince.
Then the unhappy lord implored me,
for your honor, to do a hero's deed:
to risk my life in rushing waters,
win glory; he promised me reward.
2135 I found then, as is widely known, the fierce
and dreadful guardian of the depths.
There for some time we fought hand-to-hand;
the mere surged with blood, and I severed
in that war-hall Grendel's mother's head
2140 with a mighty sword. Not easily

did I escape, but I was not then doomed;
and Halfdane's son, the lord of heroes,
once again gave me many treasures.

    "The king thus followed noble custom: XXXI
in no way was I unrewarded   2145
for my deeds of might, but Halfdane's son
showered treasure on me, as I chose;
these I wish to offer you, o king,
as show of my good will. All my joys
still are fixed on you: I have few   2150
close kinsmen except, my Hyglac, you."

    Then he had brought in the boar-banner,   *Beowulf and Hyglac*
towering war-helmet, gray corselet,   *Exchange Gifts*
and splendid sword; then he made this speech:
"When Hrothgar gave me this battle-gear,   2155
the wise prince bade me, in a few words,
to tell you something of its history:
he said it had been the Scylding king's,[79]
Heorogar's, who had it a long time,   2160
yet who would not pass the armor on
to his brave son Heoroweard, though he
was loyal to him. Use it all well!"
    I heard that four bay horses followed *Intrusive narrator*
that treasure: swift, alike, and tawny
as apples; he gave him both horses   2165
and treasure. Thus kinsmen ought to act—
not weave nets of evil for each other   *Kin-killing*
with dark craft, plotting the death of close
companions. To battle-proud Hyglac
his nephew proved himself most loyal,   2170
and each mindful of the other's good.

79. Lines 2158–62] See the genealogical chart of the Danish dynasty
in the Genealogical Tables. Son did not necessarily succeed father in
Germanic tribal kingdoms, and here Heorogar evidently preferred to
pass on the royal mantle to his younger brother Hrothgar.

I heard that he gave Hygd the neck-ring,
that wondrous treasure which Queen Wealhtheow
had given him, together with three sleek
2175 horses with bright saddles; then Hygd's breast
was honored when she received the ring.

Thus Ecgtheow's son showed himself brave,
a man known in war for noble deeds,
who acted honorably; he never slew
2180 his drinking comrades, nor was cruel in heart,
but the ample gift God had given him,
the greatest of human strengths, he used
bravely in battle. Long had he been[80]
despised: the Geats showed him no respect,
2185 nor would the lord of the Weders honor
him with many gifts on the mead-bench;
but they felt strongly he was slothful
and cowardly. Yet change came, an end
to all the famous man's afflictions.

2190 Then the heroes' keeper, the brave king,
bade that Hrethel's heirloom be brought in,[81]
covered with gold; among the Geats then
there was no finer treasure in sword's form.
He laid that in Beowulf's lap, and gave
2195 to him seven thousand hides of land,[82]
a hall and throne. Together they held
in that nation inherited land,
ancestral rights, though the spacious realm
itself was for him of higher rank.

80. Lines 2183–89] There is no other reference to Beowulf's slug-
gish youth. This passage seems to reflect the folk-tale motif of the
"youngest brother" who, despised as worthless, succeeds in a quest
after his older brothers have failed; but see the Introduction for another view of the propriety of the passage.
81. Hrethel's heirloom] The sword (l. 2193) that had belonged to
"the brave king" Hyglac's father, Hrethel.
82. The equivalent of the size of North Mercia, a considerable area.

In turn it happened in later days,   *Beowulf and the Dragon*
after the clash of war killed Hyglac,
and war-swords slaughtered his son Heardred
beneath the shelter of his shield
when those bold fighters, the Battle-Scylfings,[83]
sought him out and cruelly assailed   2205
Hereric's nephew in his own nation—
after that time the broad kingdom came
into Beowulf's hands. He ruled it well
for fifty years—a venerable king
and homeland guardian—till one began   2210
his own rule on dark nights: a dragon,
who guarded a hoard on the high heath
in a steep stone mound, whose entrance stood
beneath, to men unknown. But some man
crept within close to the heathen hoard,   2215
seized in hand a large and costly cup.
Later the dragon learned of his loss,
though sleeping he'd been at first deceived
by the thief's cunning; then those close by
in the nation came to know his rage.   2220
     Neither by design nor by desire   *The Theft*   XXXII
did the culprit dare the dragon's hoard,   *of a Cup from the Hoard*
but for dire necessity the slave
of some one of men fled hostile blows,
and, in need of refuge, the sinful wretch   2225
found his way within there. [Once he saw[84]

83. Battle-Scylfings] The -Scylfings were the Swedish dynasty—see
the Genealogical Tables.
84. The MS is badly damaged at ll. 2226–31; the best that can be said
about my "reconstruction" of it is that it fits the sense of the larger
context.

*The History of the
Hoard*

the sleeping worm, sudden terror struck
the unbidden guest; yet he was bold:
with rare cunning, the wretched man reached out
2230 his hand, and hurrying from the barrow, took
the studded cup.] There were many such
ancient treasures in that earthen house,
just as in olden days some unknown man
had hidden them there with thoughtful care:
2235 a vast legacy of treasured wealth
of a noble race. Death had robbed them all
of life in former times, and the lone
survivor of that band, saddened by
the loss of friends, felt the same fate close:
2240 knew he had but little time to use
the long-held treasure. A barrow lay
prepared on a plain near the sea–waves,
new–built on the bluff, of hard access;
the guardian of rings bore plated gold
2245 within there, all the tribal treasure
worth the hoarding. He spoke but few words:
"Hold now, earth, what warriors cannot,
the wealth of heroes! Lo! it was yours
before good men obtained it from you.
2250 Through war, dread and evil death has claimed
my people: each one has passed from life,
from joy in the hall. I have no one
to carry sword or clean the costly
plated cup: the company is gone.
2255 The hard, gold-ornamented helmet
must lose its plates; the polishers sleep
whose task it was to shine the war-mask;
so too the war-coat, which once endured
the bite of swords over crashing shields,
2260 decays with the man. Nor can ring-mail
travel far and wide with the war-lord,

by heroes' sides. No harp-joy sounds
from unplucked strings, no good hawk swings
through the hall, no swift horse stamps his feet
in the courtyard: baleful death has come   2265
and swept far off many living men!"
    Thus sad of mind, he mourned in his grief,
one outlasting all, wandering joyless
both day and night, till death reached out
and touched his heart.   2270
                      The ancient ravager   *The Dragon's Revenge*
found the glorious hoard unguarded: *for the Theft*
the smooth-skinned fire-dragon who seeks out
barrows and, breathing flames, flies at night
maliciously; men on earth greatly
fear him. His fate it is to seek out[85]   2275
treasure in the ground, guard heathen gold
till old in years, though it yields him nothing.
    Thus the people's scourge secured in earth
a huge and mighty treasure-house
three hundred winters, until one man   2280
enraged him, he who bore to his lord
the plated cup, sought peace-conditions
for himself. Thus the hoard was ransacked,
its wealth diminished, and pardon won
for the fugitive; for the first time   2285
his lord looked upon men's work of old.
    Then the worm awoke, and new strife with it.
Stouthearted, it slithered over stones,
found its foe's footprint: he'd stepped forward
cunningly, close to the dragon's head.   2290
—Thus an undoomed man can easily
survive woe and misery, if he

85. Lines 2275–76] It was proverbial that dragons guarded buried treasure; cf. the OE *Maxims II*: "a dragon must occupy a barrow, old, exulting in treasures."

has God's grace!—The guardian of the hoard
searched the ground, eager to spy the man
2295   who had harmed him sorely while he slept.
In furious rage he went round and round
outside the mound, but there was no man
in that waste. Yet thoughts of war filled him
with battle-joy. At times he turned back
2300   to the cave, sought this or that precious cup,
and straightway knew someone had disturbed
his treasured gold. The guardian of the hoard
waited restless until dusk arrived:
bursting with rage, the barrow-keeper
2305   wished to requite his foe with dire flame
for the dear cup's theft. Then daylight passed,
to the worm's delight: no longer would
he wait on barrow wall, but burning
bright with flame sailed off. Fear gripped the Geats
2310   as he began, and their treasure-giver
quickly found the end a sad affair.

XXXIII   Then that strange visitor spewed forth flames,
burned bright dwellings; flickering fires brought
horror to men. The hateful airborne beast
2315   wished to leave nothing there alive.
The hostile worm's violence in war
was evident everywhere to all:
how the destroyer hated and hurt
the Geats. He darted back to his hoard
2320   and secret splendid hall before day came.
He had ringed those living in the land
with flame and fire; had faith in his strength
and barrow wall: that hope deceived him.

Beowulf Seeks Revenge   Then Beowulf at once had word truly
on the Dragon   of that horror, for his own home,
best of buildings and gift-throne of the Geats,
had melted in leaping flames; fierce grief

and anguish of mind racked the good man:
the wise king thought he'd greatly angered
2330		God, the Eternal Lord, by breaking
natural law; dark thoughts gnawed at his breast,[86]
which was not customary with him.

       The fire-dragon with his flames had razed
the Geats' defences: inland fortress
2335		and coastal strongholds; the Weders' king,
keen for war, devised revenge for this.
Then the heroes' lord, the warriors' hope,
bade a wondrous battle-shield be made
all of iron; he was well aware
2340		no shield of linden-wood would last
against the flame. Yet the long-famed prince
was destined to end his fleeting days
of worldly life—and the worm with him,
though he long held the hoarded wealth.
2345		Then the princely giver of rings scorned
to seek the flying beast with a large band
of fighting men: combat held no fear
for him, nor did he value highly
the worm's war-might and valor; for he
2350		had braved and lived through many battles,
hostile clashes, since he had cleansed
Hrothgar's hall, victorious had crushed
the life from that loathsome race, Grendel
and his kin.

Poet's Account of Hyglac's Frisian Raid and Swedish-Geatish Wars

       Not the least encounter[87]
hand-to-hand occurred when Hyglac fell:

86. natural law] The OE *ofer ealde riht* "against the old law"—most critics nowadays interpret this as "natural moral law" which, according to St. Paul, even the good pagan could discover without Christian revelation.

87. Lines 2354–59] The second reference to Hyglac's ill-fated Frisian raid; see ll. 1202–14, and further references in ll. 2501–8 and 2913–21.

when Hrethel's son, the Geatish king, was slain
in battle by blood-thirsting sword-strokes:
when the dear lord of the people perished
among the Frisians. By his own might
Beowulf got away safely to sea;   2360
he bore in his arms the battle-gear[88]
of thirty men when he moved seaward.
The Hetware who'd borne shields against him[89]
had no need at all to boast about
that fight on foot: few returned to seek   2365
their homes from battle with that hero!
Then Ecgtheow's son swam the sea's expanse,
returning home wretched and alone;
there Hygd offered him the hoard and realm,
rings and royal throne, not trusting that   2370
her son could hold their ancestral seat,
with Hyglac dead, against invading hosts.
By no means, for all their misery,
could the people persuade the prince
that he should become Heardred's lord and king,   2375
or choose to put on royal power;
but he guided him with good counsel
and gracious friendship, till he grew up
and ruled the Geats.

Exiles sought refuge[90]

88. Lines 2361–62] Whether Beowulf actually towed this battle-gear
(whatever it consisted of) with him when he "swam the sea's expanse" (l. 2367) has been hotly debated; some even doubt that he
swam back to Geatland, preferring to interpret the words as meaning he rowed a small boat.
89. Hetware] A tribe allied with the Frisians.
90. Lines 2379–96] This is the first of three (or four) accounts of the
Swedish-Geatish wars; cf. ll. 2472–89 and ll. 2923–88 (and ll.
2610–19). The episode alluded to here is chronologically the last
phase of the feud (except for the renewal prophesied by the messenger in ll. 2922–23 and 2999–3001). Ohthere's sons, Eanmund and
Eadgils, rebelled against their uncle Onela, king of the Swedes, and

2380   with Heardred over the sea: Ohthere's sons,
        who had rebelled against the best
        of sea-kings giving gold in Sweden:
        Onela, a famous prince, protector
        of the Scylfings. His hospitality
2385   cost Hyglac's son his life: he received
        a mortal wound from a well-aimed sword.
        And Ongentheow's son sought his home
        once again when Heardred lay lifeless;
        he let Beowulf hold the royal throne
2390   and rule the Geats: that was a good king.

XXXIV   In later days he recalled the death
        of his prince: he befriended the hapless
        Eadgils, supporting Ohthere's son
        across the wide sea with warriors
2395   and weapons; and gained revenge when he,
        with cold attack, killed King Onela.

                Thus Ecgtheow's son had survived every
        encounter and dangerous conflict,
        each courageous deed, till that one day
2400   when he was to fight against the worm.
        Swollen with anger, the lord of the Geats
        went, one of twelve, to view the dragon;
        he had found out whence the feud arose,
        so cruel to men: the celebrated cup
2405   had come to him through the thief's own hand.
        That wretched slave, who first caused the strife,
        made up the thirteenth member of that

-----

sought refuge among the Geats, whose hospitality cost Hyglac's son
Heardred, as well as Eanmund, his life, and brought Beowulf to the
Geatish throne. On the killing of Eanmund in this struggle, see ll.
2610–19. Ohthere and Onela were the sons of Ongentheow (l. 2387),
whose death is recounted in ll. 2484–88 and 2949–81; it is generally
thought that Ohthere was the elder son and preceded Onela on the
throne.

company; disconsolate, he had
to guide them, going against his will
to where he knew the hidden earth-hall stood,   2410
a lone barrow by the surging sea's
pounding waves, full of filigree work
and gold chains. The frightful guardian,
old and combat-ready, kept the gold
treasures under ground: no easy bargain   2415
was it for any one to obtain!
Then the war-brave king sat on the cliff;
the gold-friend of the Geats wished good luck
to his comrades. His mind was mournful,
restless, ripe for death; very near now   2420
was the fate come to fetch the old man's
treasured soul, to sunder sharply life
from body: the prince's spirit would not
much longer be confined in flesh.

    Beowulf, Ecgtheow's son, spoke out boldly: *Beowulf's Account of*
"In my youth I endured many combats,   *Geatish Dynasty,*
many wars; all those I remember.   *Swedish-Geatish Wars,*
I was seven when the people's prince   *and Hyglac's Frisian*
and treasure-lord took me from my father;   *Raid*
King Hrethel kept and guarded me, gave   2430
me wealth and feast, mindful of kinship:
while he lived, he loved me as no less
a warrior in court than any son—
Herebeald, Hæthcyn, or my own Hyglac.
A deathbed for the eldest was laid out   2435
accidently by his kinsman's deed:
Hæthcyn felled his friendly lord-to-be
with an arrow from his horn-tipped bow;   *kin-killing*
he missed his mark and hit his kinsman,
brother killing brother with bloody shaft.   2440
That wicked crime could not be requited:
though numbing heart and mind, Herebeald's loss

call for payment or revenge.

s it for an old man sorrowful [91]

e that his son should ride young

allows: he voices his grief

wful song when his son hangs

raven's joy and he can find

ɔ for him for all his years' wisdom.

lawn reports his son's departure

nere; he does not care to await

rival of another heir

s stronghold when the first has found

leeds ending in enforcèd death.

rowful, he sees in his son's dwelling

the empty wine-hall, waste and cheerless,

where winds only rest: riders, warriors,

sleep in their graves; no harp resounds,

no mirth fills the courts as formerly.

XXXV   2460   Then he takes to bed, sings a dirge for

his only son: all seemed too spacious,

fields and home.

So was it for Hrethel,

carrying in his heart for Herebeald

swelling grief; there was no ground to take

2465   for settling the feud with his slayer:

he could not hate Hæthcyn for the hostile

dire deed, though he was not dear to him.

That sorrow proved too heavy for him:

he gave up men's joys and chose God's light,

2470   and left his sons, as prosperous men do,

lands and strongholds when he left this life.

91. Lines 2444–62] Just as Hrethel could not exact revenge or *wergild* (the stipulated payment for the wrongful death of a warrior) from his own son Hæthcyn, so, according to Anglo-Saxon law, a man put to death for crimes could not be avenged or payment exacted for him.

"Then across wide water conflict flared,
strife between Swedes and Geats stemming from
common hatred, after Hrethel died
and Ongentheow's sons, bold and active   2475
in fighting, would not keep their friendship
over the sea, but often savagely
attacked our host near Hreosnabeorh.[92]
My friends and kinsmen avenged that feud[93]
and outrage of war, as is well known,   2480
though one brother bought it with his life—
a hard bargain: battle was fatal
to Hæthcyn, the Geats' lord and leader.
Then, I heard, his kinsman on the morrow
took vengeance with sword's edge on his slayer, 2485
once Ongentheow sought out Eofor:[94]
his war-helmet split, the old Scylfing
fell, blood-drained; for Eofor's hand, recalling
bloody deeds, did not check its deadly stroke.

"As fate consented, I served Hyglac   2490
well in war with my bright sword, repaid
treasures, land, hereditary home
he conferred on me. He had no need
to seek less worthy warrior, reward
with gifts such a one from the Gifthas,[95]   2495
from the Spear-Danes, or from Sweden;
I marched before him in the foot-troops,
always in the vanguard, and ever shall
thus wage battle while this sword, which has

92. Hreosnabeorh] A hill in Geatland.
93. Lines 2479–89] The scene of the Geats' attack is Sweden, near
Ravenswood (l. 2925), and that battle, in which Hæthcyn of the
Geats and the Swedish king Ongentheow fall, is given in detail in ll.
2923–88.
94. Eofor] Hyglac's thane, who kills Ongentheow; see ll. 2962–81.
95. Gifthas] An East Germanic tribe.

Beowulf

2500 for long duly served me, shall endure—
since with my hands before the hosts[96]
I slew Dæghrefn, the Hugas' champion:[97]
not at all could he carry armor,
breast-ornaments, to the Frisian king,
2505 but that brave, noble standard-bearer
fell in battle; no blade's edge killed him,
but my hand-grip crushed his pulsing heart,
broke his body. Now, however, both
hand and hard sword must fight for the hoard."

The Dragon's First Assault

      Beowulf spoke once more, made battle-boast
the last time: "I undertook in youth
to engage in many wars; still I wish,
old guardian of my folk, to seek feud,
do a great deed, if the evil-doer
2515 will come from his earth-hall out to me."

      He greeted each warrior one last time,
addressed his dear companions, those brave
helmet-bearers: "I would not bear sword,
weapon, to the worm, if I knew how else
2520 I might grapple with the fearful foe
proudly, as with Grendel long ago;
but I expect blistering battle-fire,
poisonous breath. Therefore I bear a shield,
wear my mail-shirt. Not one foot will I
2525 flee from the barrow-keeper; but fate,
which measures every man, must decide
between us by this wall. My will is firm:
I boast no further against the beast.
Wait on the barrow, warriors safely

96. Lines 2501–8] The third reference to Hyglac's Frisian raid; cf. ll. 1202–14, 2354–59, and 2913–21. Dæghrefn, l. 2502, was presumably the slayer of Hyglac, whose death, Beowulf here suggests, he fully avenged.
97. Hugas] I.e., the Frisians.

clad in armor, to see which of us two 2530
after the blaze of battle better
survives wounds. It is not your venture,
nor any man's measure save mine alone,
to match his might with the fearful foe's,
to do this heroic deed. By daring 2535
shall I gain the gold, or dire battle,
ending life, will take your lord away!"
    The famed warrior stood up by his shield;
brave, helmeted, he bore his mail-coat
beneath stone cliffs, trusted in the strength 2540
of one man: such is no coward's way!
The splendid warrior, who had survived
many conflicts and battle-clashes
where foot-troops fought, saw then by the wall
a stone arch standing, through which a stream 2545
burst out from the barrow, boiling hot
with deadly fire; he could not endure
for long in the hollow near the hoard
unscorched because of the dragon's flame.
Enraged, the man of the Weder-Geats 2550
let a battle cry fly from his breast,
stouthearted shouted, voice roaring in
under the gray stone, clear call to battle.
Hatred stirred, the hoard-guardian had heard
the voice of man; there was no more time 2555
to ask for peace. First issued forth
from out the stone the fearful foe's breath,
hot battle-steam; the ground resounded.
Below the barrow, the Geatish lord
swung his shield up toward the strange terror. 2560
Then the coiled creature's heart impelled it
to seek combat; the good war-king
had drawn his sword, an ancient heirloom
not dull of edge: each wished to destroy

2565 the other, yet stood in awe of him.
With firm heart the friend and lord of men
stood by his tall shield, strong in armor,
while the worm quickly coiled itself up.
Then, coiled and flaming, it swept forward,
2570 hastening to its fate. And for less time
than he had hoped, the shield protected
life and body of the famous lord:
there, for the first time, he had to fend
for himself without fate granting him
2575 undiluted glory. The Geats' lord
raised his hand, so struck the gleaming horror
with his ancient sword that its bright edge
met bone, gave way, and bit less deeply
than the people's king had need, hard-pressed
2580 in distress. After that battle-stroke
the barrow-guardian's heart grew savage;
he spewed deadly fire: war-flames spread wide.
The gold-friend of the Geats could not boast
of sweet victory: his bare sword failed
2585 in battle, as the good ancient blade
ought not have done. No easy journey
was it for Ecgtheow's famous son
to give ground, give up the earthly plain:
against his will he had to settle
2590 elsewhere, even as every man must
leave this fleeting life.

The Second Assault: It was not long
Flight of the Retainers   before the fearsome foes met again.
The hoard-guardian took heart, once again
breathed fiercely, and he who ruled the folk
2595 suffered great distress, engulfed in flames.
Nor did his comrades, hand-chosen sons
of nobles, stand about him in a band
as warriors should, but fled to the wood,

saved their lives. Only one man's heart surged
with sorrow: nothing can set aside   2600
kinship's claims for one who thinks rightly!
        Wiglaf was he called, Weohstan's son,[98]   *Wiglaf*   XXXVI
a worthy shield-warrior, a Scylfing,   *Comes to Beowulf's Aid*
Ælfhere's kinsman. Seeing his liege-lord
suffer from the heat under his helmet,   2605
he recalled honors he'd given him,
the rich dwelling of the Wægmundings,
property rights his father had possessed;
he could not hold back: his hand seized shield,
yellow linden-wood, drew the ancient sword   2610
said to be the heirloom of Eanmund,
Ohthere's son. Weohstan had slain him,
a friendless exile, with the sword's edge
in battle, and brought Eanmund's uncle
his shining helmet, his linked mail-shirt,   2615
old giant-sword. Onela gave him[99]
all of his kinsman's war-equipment,
ready battle-gear—raised no question
of feud, though he'd felled his brother's son.
Weohstan saved that gear many seasons,   2620
the sword and mail-shirt, till his son could
perform brave deeds, as his old father had;
he gave him—they lived then with the Geats—
countless war-garments when he passed on,

98. Lines 2602–3—Scylfing] Wiglaf is here said to be a Swede, and
we see in ll. 2612–19 that his father had indeed fought on the Swedish
side in the battle in which Heardred, Hyglac's son, was killed (see
note to ll. 2379–96), and Weohstan himself had killed Eanmund, the
rebellious nephew of Onela. Yet Weohstan's and Wiglaf's family is
the Wægmundings, Beowulf's own kindred (see ll. 2813–14), and at
Weohstan's death they evidently were among the Geats (see l. 2623).
It was not unusual for warrior clans to switch their tribal loyalties.
99. Lines 2616–19] Since Onela wished his rebellious nephew dead,
he rewarded his slayer rather than exacting vengeance or monetary
compensation (*wergild*) from him.

2625 old, from life's path. Now was the first time
that the young champion should face the charge
of battle beside his noble lord.
His courage did not melt, nor kinsman's
heirloom fail, in war: the worm discovered
2630 that, once they had come together.
    Wiglaf spoke, said many fitting words
to his companions, his mind mournful:
"I remember the time we took mead
in the beer-hall, and boldly promised
2635 our lord, who gave us all these treasures,
we would repay him for the war-gear,
the helmets and hard swords, if such need
befell him. Therefore of his own will
he chose us above all for this venture,
2640 thought us war-worthy, and gave me these gifts,
because he judged us adept with spears,
bold in wearing helmets; though our lord,
the people's protector, intended
to perform this valorous feat alone,
2645 because he, of all men, had gained most
fame in daring deeds. That day is come
when our liege-lord could use the strength
of good warriors; let us go to him,
help our war-leader while this heat lasts,
2650 grim fire-terror. As for me, God knows
I would much prefer the flame embrace
my body beside my gold-giver.
It seems wrong to me that we bear shields
freely home again, unless we first
2655 can fell the foe and defend the life
of the Weders' prince. I know full well
it is not his desert that he should,
alone of the Geatish host, suffer,
sink in combat. Now sword and helmet,

mail-coat, war-gear, must be our common lot."   2660
    Then he strode through the deadly steam,
helmeted, to help his lord; said little:
"Dear Beowulf, perform all well, just as
long since, in your youthful days, you said
that while you lived you would never let   2665
your glory fail. Now, prince famed for deeds,
be resolute and protect your life
with all your might; I shall help you."
    After these words, the worm came angry:
the dread, hateful foe surged bright with flames   2670
a second time toward his enemies,
hated men. Hot flames advanced in waves:
the shield burnt to the boss, the mail-shirt
was useless to the young spear-warrior;
yet the youth quickly covered himself   2675
with his kinsman's shield when flames consumed
his own. Then the war-king again recalled
his glory, struck with such great strength
and violence that his sword stuck fast
in the beast's head—and shattered: Beowulf's   2680
gray heirloom sword, Nægling, deserted him
in the fight. It was his misfortune
that swords' blades were powerless to aid
him in battle: too strong was that hand
which, I've been told, overtaxed all swords   2685
with its stroke; however hard the weapon
steeled in wounds, it helped him not at all.
    Then still a third time the people's scourge,   *The Third Assault*
dread fire-dragon, was mindful of feuds;
when he had room, he rushed the brave man;   2690
hot and battle-fierce, he pierced his neck
with his bitter teeth; Beowulf was bathed
in his life's blood, which flowed out in waves.
    Then at the need of the nation's king   XXXVII

2695 the loyal thane revealed the valor,
skill, and boldness which were his by birth.
The brave man paid no heed to the head,
but burned his hand helping his kinsman
as, armor-clad, he struck the cruel foe
2700 somewhat lower down, so that his sword,
bright, adorned, plunged in, and the fire began
to subside. Then the king himself still
ruled his wits, drew the razor-sharp knife
meant for slaughter from his coat of mail,
2705 and slashed the worm straight through the middle.
They had felled the foe—valor drove out
its life: both high-born kinsmen had cut
it down together. So should a thane do
at need!
                         For his lord, that was the last
2710 victory he achieved in the world,
the last work of his will. For the wound
the earth-dragon earlier gave him
began to burn and swell; he straightway
found the poison welling in fierce rage
2715 within his breast. Then the wise prince went
till he sat on a seat by the wall;
he gazed at the work of giants, saw
how, within, the eternal earth-hall held
stone arches supported on pillars.
2720 The thane immeasurably good then
bathed by hand his blood-smeared famous prince
with water where he sat battle-weary,
and undid his dear lord's helmet.
              Beowulf spoke—he spoke despite his hurt,
2725 his mortal wound; he was well aware
he had reached the end of his time on earth
and happiness; passed was the number
of his days, death immeasurably near:

"Now I should wish to give my war-gear
to my son, had any such heir, seed   2730
of my flesh, been granted me by fate
to succeed me. I have ruled the Geats
for fifty years; there was no folk-king
from any neighboring tribe who dared
with his cohorts attack me in war,   2735
assail me with terror. I awaited
at home what fate brought, held my own well,
sought no treacherous quarrels nor swore oaths
deceitfully. Now, sick with death-wounds,
I can still have joy in all those things;   2740
for the Ruler of men need not charge me
with murder of kinsmen when my life
quits my body. Now go quickly
under the gray stone to survey the hoard,
dear Wiglaf, now that the worm lies dead,   2745
sleeps sore wounded, bereft of treasure.
Make haste now, so that I may clearly
view the ancient wealth, the gold and bright
strange gems, so that, seeing all that wealth,
I may more easily yield up my life   2750
and the realm which I have ruled so long."

Then, I heard, Weohstan's son speedily   *The*   XXXVIII
obeyed the words of his battle-sick,   *Treasure Is Viewed;*
wounded lord, went under the barrow's roof   *Beowulf's Death*
still wearing his woven shirt of mail.   2755
When the brave, triumphant young retainer
passed the seat, he saw many splendid
jewels and gold glittering on the ground,
wonders on the wall, and the worm's den;
the old dusk-flier's cave held cups stripped   2760
of ornaments, bowls of men of old
lacking polishers. There lay many
old and rusty helmets, and arm-rings

twisted skillfully. (Treasure can tempt
2765 any man easily, gold lying
in the ground—heed this, whoever will!) [100]
Also he saw high over the hoard
an all-gold banner hanging, greatest
of woven handiworks; a light shone
2770 from it, so that he could see the floor,
survey the treasure. There was no trace
of the worm there: the sword had slain him.
Then I heard how one man in the mound
rifled the hoard, relics of giants:
2775 loaded his arms with goblets and plates
as he wished, likewise took the standard,
brightest of banners. The old lord's sword,
with its iron edge, had already
killed the creature who so long guarded
2780 the treasure, kept the terror of flame
hot for the hoard's sake, rising fiercely
in the dead of night till he died.

 Wiglaf hurried, eager to return
enriched with treasure; his heart was troubled,
2785 anxious whether he would find the lord
of the Geats, his strength gone, still alive
in the place he'd previously left him.
Then, treasure-laden, he found his lord,
the famed prince, his blood still pouring out,
2790 at his life's end; once more he laved him
with water, till words began to break
out from his breast-hoard.

 [Then Beowulf spoke],
old and suffering—surveyed the gold:
"With these words I give thanks to God,

---

100. heed] The OE verb I have thus translated is more usually taken
as "hide"; either meaning is possible—or plausible.

the King of Glory, the Eternal Lord,   2795
for all the treasures I stare at here,
that I could acquire for my people
such a fortune before my death-day.
Now that I have sold my old life-span
for the treasure-hoard, you must attend   2800
the nation's needs; I can stay no longer.
Bid battle-famed men make a bright mound
on the ocean's cape after the pyre:
a remembrance for my people,
it shall tower high on Hronesness,   2805
so that seafarers then shall call it
'Beowulf's Barrow'—those who steer tall ships
from afar over the darkling seas."
The brave king took the gold collar
from his neck, and handed to his thane,   2810
the young spear-hero, his gold helmet,
collar, and mail-coat; bade him use them well:
"You are the last of our family,
the Wægmundings; fate has swept away
all my kinsmen, courageous warriors,   2815
to their final doom; I must follow."
Those were the old man's last words and thoughts
before taking his place on the pyre
with its hot battle-flames; from his breast
his soul went to seek the doom of the just.   2820

      For the young man it was a moment   [XXXIX]
of great sorrow, seeing him he best
loved lying on earth at his life's end,
wretchedly slain. Likewise his slayer,
the dread earth-dragon, bereft of life,   2825
lay stretched out, overcome. No longer
could the coiled worm rule the hoard of rings,
for blades of iron, the battle-sharp
hard legacy of hammers, slew it,

2830 so that the wide-flier, stilled by wounds,
      tumbled to earth near the treasure house.
      Not at all would he fly through the air
      to appear in the dead of night, proud
      of precious wealth, but he fell to earth
2835 through the work of the war-leader's hand.
      Indeed, no man of might in that land,
      so I've heard, however daring he
      might be in deeds, could battle the breath
      of that venomous foe successfully,
2840 or disturb the ring-hoard with his hands,
      if he encountered the barrow-keeper
      waiting, awake. Beowulf paid with death
      for his share of that lordly treasure:
      each of them had reached the end of this
2845 fleeting life.

The Return of the   It was not long before
Cowards   the ten cowards came out of the wood
      together, false traitors to their oaths,
      who had feared to bring to battle-play
      their spears at their liege-lord's greatest need;
2850 but they bore, shameful, shields and armor
      to the place where their aged leader lay.
      They looked at Wiglaf; he sat wearied,
      foot-warrior by the war-lord's shoulders,
      trying to wake him with water—in vain.
2855 He might not, however much he wished,
      keep his chieftain alive on this earth,
      nor alter aught of the Ruler's judgment:
      God's decree would control the deeds
      of every man, as it still does now.
2860   Then grim answer easily came from
      the forlorn youth to those lacking courage;
      Wiglaf, Weohstan's son, spoke out clearly—
      heartsick, he looked at the unloved ones:

"Lo, he who will speak truly can say
that the liege-lord who gave you treasures,   2865
that war-equipment in which you stand—
when on the ale-bench the prince often
gave to his thanes sitting in the hall
helmets and mail-coats, the most splendid
he could find anywhere, far or near—   2870
that he quite threw away that war-gear
to his grief when war once engulfed him.
The nation's king had no need to boast
of war-comrades; yet God, Who controls
all victories, allowed him to avenge   2875
himself single-handed when courage
was called for. I could little protect
his life in that strife, yet strove to help
my kinsman beyond my measure of strength:
when I struck the deadly foe with sword,   2880
it grew weaker, fire welled less swiftly
from its head. Too few defenders thronged
around the prince when peril pressed him.
Now shall treasure-getting and sword-giving,
pleasure in property for your kin,   2885
and all other comforts cease. Each man
of your clan must forfeit his land-right,
wander in exile, once nobles learn
from afar of your cowardly flight,
inglorious deed. Death is better   2890
for every warrior than living shame!"
    Then he bade the battle-news be told
in the stronghold beyond the headland,
where the shield-bearing warrior-band sat
sad in mind the morning long, expecting
either their dear lord's last day or
his return. He who rode up the bluff
was not long silent about his news,

The Messenger's   XL
Account of Hyglac's
Frisian Raid and the
Swedish-Geatish Wars

but spoke aloud truthfully to all:

2900 "Now he who gave our people joy,
lord of the Weder-Geats, lies slaughtered
on his deathbed by the dragon's deeds;
beside him lies his life-enemy,
sick to death with knife-wounds: with his sword

2905 he could not inflict the fearful foe
with wound in any way. Wiglaf sits
by Beowulf; Weohstan's warrior son
watches over his unliving lord,
with heavy heart keeps constant vigil

2910 over friend and foe.
                                    Now our people
must expect times of strife, once the fall
of our king becomes manifest
to Franks and Frisians.
                                    A bitter feud[101]
was forged with the Hugas when Hyglac

2915 came with a fleet into Frisian land
where the Hetware humbled him in war,[102]
quickly with a much stronger force, caused
the mailed warrior to bow low and fall
among foot-troops rather than give treasures

2920 as lord to his retainers. Since then
the Franks' king's favor has not been ours.[103]

        "Nor do I expect peace or faith
from the Swedish nation, for widely known[104]
is it that Ongentheow took the life

101. Lines 2913–21] This is the fourth and final account of Hyglac's
Frisian raid (cf. ll. 1202–14, 2354–59, and 2501–8).
102. Hetware] A tribe allied with the Frisians; cf. l. 2363.
103. The OE text refers here to the "Merovingian's favor"; the Mer-
ovingians were a Frankish dynasty, and the term probably had become generic for the Frankish rulers.
104. Lines 2923–88] The last account of the Swedish-Geatish wars
(cf. ll. 2379–96 and 2479–89).

of Hæthcyn, Hrethel's son, near Ravenswood,   2925
when the Geats in all their arrogance
first assailed the Swedes, the War-Scylfings:
at once Ohthere's wise and terrible
old father gave Hæthcyn a counterblow,
cut down the sea-leader, rescued his wife,   2930
mother of Onela and Ohthere,
the old queen, stripped of gold ornaments;
and then hunted down his deadly foes,
till they escaped with difficulty
to Ravenswood, bereft of their lord.   2935
With a large force he besieged the swords'
weary, wounded remnant; promised woes
to the hapless troop all through the night:
said that, come dawn, he would cut them down
with sword blades, hang some on gallows-trees   2940
as sport for the birds. But with daybreak
comfort came to those heavyhearted
when they heard the sound of Hyglac's horn
and trumpet as that hero traveled
with his hand-picked host along their path.   2945
    "Widely seen was the bloody swath cut   XLI
by the savage fight of Swedes and Geats,
how those peoples roused feud between them.
Then the brave old warrior Ongentheow,
mourning much, pulled back with his kinsmen,   2950
seeking his fortress further away:
he had heard of proud Hyglac's battle-
prowess, did not trust he could resist
the sea-men's might, protect his treasure,
sons, and wife against the war-sailors;   2955
old, he turned from there to the safety
of his earth-wall. Pursuit was offered
then to the Swedes, and Hyglac's standards
went forth over that field of refuge

2960   once the Hrethlings breached the citadel.
There gray-haired Ongentheow was brought to bay
by sword blades, so that the people's king
had to submit to fate as Eofor
decreed. Wulf, son of Wonred, had struck
2965   Ongentheow so fiercely with sword
that at that stroke blood spurted forth
from under his hair. Yet the old Scylfing
was not cowed, but quickly turned on him,
and then the people's king repaid
2970   that slaughterous blow with worse exchange.
Nor could bold Wonred's son resume the fight,
give counterblow to the old warrior,
for Ongentheow had shorn his helmet through,
so that he had to bow down, bloodstained.
2975   He fell to earth, not yet doomed to death:
he recovered, though the wound hurt him.
When his brother fell, Hyglac's brave thane
Eofor let his broad sword, an old blade
made by giants, break the giant helmet
2980   across the shield-wall; the king went down,
the people's keeper, stricken mortally.
Many men bound Eofor's brother's wounds,
quickly lifted him when time allowed
and they controlled the battlefield.
2985   Meanwhile one warrior stripped the other:
Eofor took Ongentheow's iron-mail,
hard, hilted sword, and his helmet, too,
carried the old man's arms to Hyglac.
He received that treasure, and swore he'd
2990   give him fair rewards once home; and did so.
When the lord of the Geats, Hrethel's son,
came home, he requited Eofor and Wulf
for their war-service with vast wealth,
gave each land and interlocking rings

worth one hundred thousand—no one on earth   2995
   could[105]
belittle the reward they'd won by their fame;
and he gave Eofor, as pledge of favor,
his sole daughter to adorn his home.[106]
   "That is the feud and fierce enmity,
mortal hate of men, for which I fear   3000
the Swedish hosts will seek to attack us
when they learn our lord is lifeless,
he who kept our treasure and kingdom
against our foes, worked the people's good
after the death of dauntless heroes,   3005
daring Scylfings, and still beyond that
did noble deeds.
           Now haste would be best:
let us look at our king lying there,
and bring him who gave us rings on his way
to the pyre. No small part of the hoard   3010
shall melt with the hero; but a huge
amount of treasure, countless gold
grimly purchased, rings paid for at the last
with his own life—these the fire shall eat,
flames enfold. No warrior shall wear   3015
ornament in memory, nor maiden
aid her beauty with bright necklaces,
but sad of mind, stripped of gold, they shall
walk on foreign ground, not once but often,
now that our leader has laid down laughter,   3020
joy, and mirth. Therefore many a spear,
morning-cold, shall be grasped in hands
and raised on high; no sound of the harp
shall wake warriors, but the dark raven,

105. one hundred thousand] I.e., of monetary units. Lines 2995–96
are hypermetric; see note to ll. 1163–68.
106. I.e., as his wife.

3025   eager for doomed men, shall speak much, telling
        the eagle how he fared at eating
        when he plundered the slain with the wolf."

Beowulf's Funeral   Thus the bold messenger made known
        the hateful news: he did not hold back
3030   events or words. The troop all arose,
        went, unhappy and with welling tears,
        under Earnaness to see the wonder.
        There they found him who in former times
        gave them rings now on his bed of rest,
3035   lifeless on the sand; the last day
        had come for the brave man: the war-king,
        the Weders' prince, had died a wondrous death.
        First they had seen a stranger creature,
        the loathsome worm, lying opposite
3040   on the plain: discolored terribly,
        the fire-dragon scorched by its own flames.[107]
        It was fifty feet long where it lay
        stretched out. Once it took joy in the air
        during the night, in turn descending
3045   to its den; now it was fast in death,
        had made its last use of earth-caverns.
        Beside it stood cups and pitchers;
        dishes lay there too, and precious swords
        eaten through by rust, having lain there
3050   in the earth's embrace a thousand years.
        That heritage possessed great power:[108]
        the gold of men of old was bound by spell,

107. Cf. l. 897, where the dragon Sigmund killed "melted in its mighty heat."
108. Lines 3051–57] In the earlier reference to the burial of the treasure by the last survivor (ll. 2231–66), there was no mention of a spell or curse. Possibly this spell had been cast in a previous burial, "before good men obtained it" (l. 2249), and this was the cause of the destruction of the lone survivor's tribe, as well as of the dragon (ll. 3058–62) and of Beowulf (see note to ll. 3074–75).

so that no man might ever reach
that ring-hall, unless God Himself,
True King of Victories, Mankind's Shield,   3055
should grant power to open the hoard
to such man He wished, as He saw fit.

    Thus it was plain it had not profited   XLII
that one who wrongly kept concealed
fine things beneath the wall: first he slew   3060
a peerless man, then paid for that feud
sorely. It is a mystery where
a renowned warrior may reach the end
of his life-span, when he can no longer
occupy the mead-hall with his kin.   3065
So it was with Beowulf when he sought
quarrels, sought the barrow's keeper: himself
did not know how he should leave this world.
So the great princes who'd put it there
had deeply cursed the hoard till doomsday,   3070
so that the man who plundered that plain
should be guilty of sin, grievously
damned to devils' shrines, fixed fast in hell-bonds,
unless he'd first, in his gold-fever,[109]
gained God's favor, Who possesses all.   3075

    Wiglaf, Weohstan's son, spoke out clearly:
"Many warriors, by the will of one,
often must suffer, as we do now.
We could not persuade our beloved prince,
the kingdom's keeper, by any counsel   3080
not to go against the gold-guardian,

109. Lines 3074–75] A *locus desperatus* for interpretation. Critics
have offered innumerable readings of these lines, where the meanings of words as well as their referents are ambiguous. The most important question for the larger interpretation of the poem is whether
or not the lines specifically refer to Beowulf, and if they do, whether
they include him or exclude him as one having "gold-fever" and suc-
cumbing to the spell.

to leave him lying where he long was,
dwelling in his den till the world's end:
he held to his high fate. The hoard is
3085   opened, hard bought; the force that brought
the king to that place was too powerful.
I was there within and looked at all
the chamber's riches when all was clear;
I had no friendly welcome to come in
3090   under the earth-wall. In haste I seized
with both my hands a huge burden
of treasures from the hoard, bore them hither
out to my king. He was yet alive
and sound of mind; old and suffering,
3095   he said many things, bade me greet you,
ordered that you build a high barrow
on the pyre's site, great and glorious,
suited to your lord's deeds, since he was
the most worthy warrior in the world
3100   while he had joy of his stronghold's wealth.
Let us hasten now another time
to see the pile of precious jewels,
wonders beneath the wall; I will guide you,
so that you can see close by enough
3105   rings and broad gold. Let the bier be made
ready quickly when we have come out,
and then let us carry our lord,
the belovèd man, where he must long
repose in the Ruler's protection."
3110   Then Weohstan's son, battle-brave warrior,
ordered many men, house-owners
and leaders of the people, to fetch
wood from afar for the pyre on which
their good lord was to be laid: "Now flame
3115   must darken, feast on this prince of warriors,
who often withstood the steel showers

of storms of arrows sped by bowstrings
over the shield-wall, when feathered shaft
eagerly aided the arrowhead."
    Indeed, the wise son of Weohstan then   3120
called forth the best thanes of the king's band
of retainers, seven together;
and the eight warriors went in under
the hostile roof; one bore in his hand
a bright-lit torch, leading the way.   3125
No lot was drawn for who should plunder
the hoard when the men saw in the hall
each portion lying unprotected,
perishing; little did any complain
that they should quickly carry out   3130
the precious treasures; also they pushed
the dragon off the cliff-wall, let wave take
the worm, flood enfold the hoard's keeper.
Then twisted gold and countless treasures
were loaded on a cart, and the king,   3135
gray-haired hero, was borne to Hronesness.
    Then the Geats prepared a pyre for him[110]   XLIII
on the earth—no petty one, indeed—
hung about with helmets, battle-shields,
bright mail-coats, as he had requested.   3140
In its midst men laid the famous prince,

110. Lines 3137–82] Part of Klaeber's note in his great edition of *Beowulf* is worth quoting: "The obsequies of Beowulf remind us in several respects of the famous funeral ceremonies of the classical epics. . . . More interesting still, certain important features are paralleled by the funeral of Attila (Jordanes [*History of the Goths*], c. 49, Par § 12), which was carried out after the Gothic fashion—the main points of difference being that Attila's body is not burned but buried, and that the mourning horsemen's songs of praise do not accompany the funeral ceremony but represent an initial, separate act of the funeral rites." Probably the horsemen are singing or uttering individual eulogies, orally composed as they ride around the mound, rather than chanting songs of praise in chorus.

lamenting their belovèd lord.
On the barrow warriors began to wake
the greatest of funeral-fires; smoke rose
3145 black above the blaze, the roaring flame
mixed with weeping—the wind died away—
till the fire had charred his frame of bone,
hot consumed his heart. Sad in spirit,
they mourned their distress, their liege-lord's death;
3150 likewise, a Geatish woman, with hair[III]
bound up, sang a lament for Beowulf,
dolefully, frequently saying
she feared hard days of mourning lay ahead,
many times of slaughter, war-terror,
3155 harm, captivity. Heaven swallowed the smoke.
      Then the people of the Weders built
a mound on the bluff, high and broad,
widely seen by travelers on the waves:
in ten days they built that monument
3160 to the brave warrior, encased in walls
the remnants of the fire, in the most
worthy structure wise men could devise.
In the barrow they set rings and gems,
all such ornaments as warlike men
3165 had earlier taken from the hoard:
they left the wealth of warriors for earth
to hold, gold in the ground, where it still lies,
as useless to men as it ever was.
Then battle-brave sons of high-born men,
3170 twelve in all, rode around the mound
to bewail their care and mourn their king,
compose sad lays and speak of the man:

111. Lines 3150–55] The "Geatish woman" as official mourner
would seem to have been traditional among Germanic tribes, though
some see this as a reference to Beowulf's widow (though we are
never told he married) or to an aged Queen Hygd, Hyglac's widow.

Sarah Higley

they praised his prowess and applauded
his brave deeds. So is it proper
3175 that a man outwardly honor his lord,
love him in his heart, when his spirit
has been led forth from his body.
Thus his hearth-companions in the host
of the Geats mourned the going of their lord:
3180 they said that of worldly kings he was
the mildest of men and the gentlest,
most kind to his people, most eager for fame.

Genealogical Tables
Glossary of Proper Names
List of Poetic Translators
Selected Bibliography

Genealogical Tables

I. DANES (Scyldings)

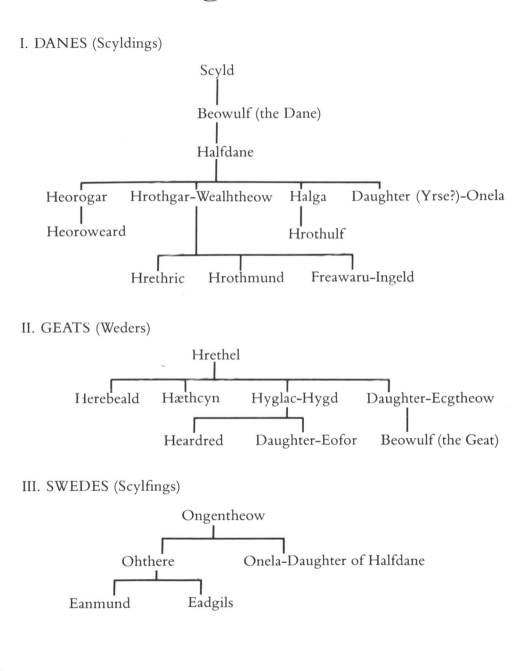

Scyld

Beowulf (the Dane)

Halfdane

Heorogar   Hrothgar–Wealhtheow   Halga   Daughter (Yrse?)–Onela

Heoroweard   Hrothulf

Hrethric   Hrothmund   Freawaru–Ingeld

II. GEATS (Weders)

Hrethel

Herebeald   Hæthcyn   Hyglac–Hygd   Daughter–Ecgtheow

Heardred   Daughter–Eofor   Beowulf (the Geat)

III. SWEDES (Scylfings)

Ongentheow

Ohthere   Onela–Daughter of Halfdane

Eanmund   Eadgils

Glossary of Proper Names

N.B. The pronunciation of Old English names, as I have modernized them somewhat for the purposes of this translation, is furnished in brackets. In most cases, the pronunciation is close to the Old English original, but not always. My symbols are self-explanatory with perhaps the following exceptions: æ=the vowel sound in Mod. E. *map*; ǣ=that of Mod. E. *add*; ʒ=that of *z* in *azure*; ð=the voiced *th*, as in *father*, whereas th=the unvoiced sound in *path*; χ=the sound of *ch* in Mod. German *ich* or *ach*. The primary stress on all names is on the first syllable.

Abel, l. 108. Biblical figure: son of Adam and Eve, killed by his brother Cain.

Ælfhere [ælf her], l. 2604. Wiglaf's kinsman.

Ashere [æsh her], ll. 1323, 1329, 1421, 2123. King Hrothgar's counselor and close companion in war; killed by Grendel's mother.

Beanstan [bǣn stän], l. 524. Breca's father; a member of the Brondings.

Beowulf [bāō wulf], passim. In ll. 17 and 53, the person referred to is Scyld Scefing's son; his name originally was probably Beow. All other references are to the Geatish hero, after whom modern editors have titled the poem; his mother was Hrethel's daughter, his father Ecgtheow.

Breca [bre kǝ], ll. 506, 531, 583. Son of Beanstan; as a youth, he engaged in a swimming match with Beowulf.

Brondings [bron dingz], l. 521. The tribe or nation of Beanstan and Breca.

Brosings [brō zingz], l. 1199. Perhaps the race of fire-dwarfs of Norse mythology (the Brisings) who made a famous necklace for the goddess Freyja.

Cain, ll. 107, 109, 1261. Biblical figure: son of Adam and Eve, who killed his brother Abel; ancestor of Grendel and his mother.

Dæghrefn [dǣi hrevn], l. 2502. The Hugas' standard-bearer and possibly Hyglac's slayer during that king's raid in Frisia; killed by Beowulf in that battle.

-Danes, passim. See Genealogical Tables. Hrothgar's people; they have many compound names (Bright-, Spear-, East-, etc.), as alliterative necessity and other considerations dictated. In l. 1090, *Danes* is used for the Half-Danes of the Finn Episode.

Eadgils [ǣd gilz], l. 2393. A member of the Scylfings (Swedes); son of Ohthere, brother of Eanmund, nephew of Onela. Gained the Swedish throne when he killed Onela.

Eanmund [ǣn mund], ll. 2611, 2614. Son of Ohthere, brother of Eadgils, nephew of Onela. Killed by Onela's warrior Weohstan, Wiglaf's father.

Earnaness [ær nŏ nes], l. 3032. "Eagles' Cliff," the headland near where Beowulf fights the dragon.

Ecglaf [edʒ läf], passim. Father of Unferth, the Danish thyle.

Ecgtheow [edʒ thāō], passim. Father of Beowulf; slayer of Heatholaf the Wylfing.

Ecgwela [edʒ welǝ], l. 1710. A Danish king who preceded Heremod.

Eofor [eo vawr], ll. 2486, 2963, 2982, 2986, 2992, 2997. Son of Wonred, brother of Wulf; slayer of King Ongentheow, the old Swedish monarch.

Eomer [āō mǝr], l. 1960. Son of King Offa of the Angles.

Ermanric [er mŏn reek], l. 1200. King of the East Goths in the late fourth century; he became a figure for tyranny in Germanic legend.

Finn [fin], ll. 1081, 1091, 1125, 1147, 1152, 1156. King of the East Frisians; husband to Hildeburh; slain by Hengest and the Half-Danes in the Finn Episode.
Fitela [fi tə lŏ], ll. 879, 889. Nephew (and son) of Sigmund, the dragon-slayer; known in Old Norse legend (*Volsungasaga*) as Sinfjotli.
Folkwalda [folk wäl də], l. 1089. Father of Finn.
Franks, ll. 1211, 2913, 2921. A West Germanic people near the Rhine; they defeated Hyglac in his raid into Frisia, c. A.D. 521.
Freawaru [frǣ wä ru], l.2023. Hrothgar's daughter; promised in marriage to Ingeld, as Beowulf reports to Hyglac.
Frisians, [fri ʒns] passim. In the Finn Episode, the East Frisians, whose king is Finn; otherwise, the West Frisians, allies of the Franks, who defeated Hyglac.
Froda [frō də], l. 2025. Father of Ingeld, king of the Heatho-beards; killed in an earlier time in feud with the Danes.

Garmund [gär mund], l. 1962. Father of King Offa of the Angles.
-Geats [geets], passim. See Genealogical Tables. Beowulf's people, a tribe that lived in Southern Sweden, south of the great lakes that separated them from their enemies the Swedes (Scylfings). Several compounds of the name appear, esp. Weder-Geats.
Gifthas [gif thəz], l. 2495. An East Germanic tribe.
Grendel [gren dl], passim. The monster who ravages Heorot for twelve years; slain by Beowulf.
Guthlaf [gūð läf], l. 1148. A Half-Dane, brother of Oslaf; follower of Hnæf and Hengest in the Finn Episode.

Hæreth [hæ rəth], l. 1927. Father of Hygd, Hyglac's queen.
Hæthcyn [hæth kin], ll. 2434, 2437, 2466, 2483, 2925. Second son of the Geat king Hrethel; accidental slayer of his elder brother Herebeald; killed by the Swedes near Ravenswood.
Halfdane [hæf dān], passim. Son of Beowulf the Dane; father of Hrothgar, etc.

Half-Danes [hæf dānz], l. 1069. In the Finn Episode, the tribe ruled by Hnæf; they are also called Danes (l. 1090) and Scyldings (l. 1154).

Halga [hä́l gə], l. 61. Younger brother of Hrothgar; father of Hrothulf.

Hama [hä́ mə], l. 1198. A figure in the Ermanric cycle of legends; his stealing of the Brosings' necklace is unique to *Beowulf.*

Handscio [hænd scō], l. 2076. The Geat warrior eaten by Grendel.

Heardred [hǽrd red], ll. 2202, 2375, 2388. Hyglac's son; after his father's death, king of the Geats; killed in battle with the Swedes, when he gave refuge to Onela's rebellious nephews Eadgils and Eanmund.

Heatho-beards [hǽ ðo beerdz], ll. 2032, 2036, 2067. N.B. Most translators give the name as Heathobards, but this suggests a false etymological connection with the word *bard;* the name probably means "Battle-beards." A Germanic tribe, possibly connected with the Langobards ("Long-beards"); apparently lived on the Continent south of the Danes, with whom they feuded; ruled by Froda and then his son Ingeld.

Heatholaf [hǽ ðo läf], l. 460. A Wylfing warrior killed by Ecgtheow, Beowulf's father.

Heatho-Rams [hǽ ðo ræmz], l. 519. A tribe living in southern Norway.

Helmings [hel mingz], l. 620. The tribe from which Queen Wealhtheow came.

Hemming [hem ming], ll. 1944, 1961. A kinsman of the fourth-century Anglian king Offa.

Hengest [heng gəst], ll. 1082, 1091, 1097, 1127. A Half-Dane warrior, Hnæf's second-in-command, who takes charge after Hnæf's death (in the Finn Episode). He may be the same as the historical Hengest (associated with Horsa) who helped found the Anglo-Saxon kingdom in Kent in A.D. 449.

Heorogar [heo ro gä́r], ll. 61, 469, 2159. Halfdane's son, Hrothgar's elder brother; he preceded Hrothgar as king of the Scyldings.

Heorot, Heort [Heo rot, Heort], passim. Hrothgar's royal hall, scene of Grendel's ravages and Beowulf's triumph. The name means "hart," and is emblematic of that royal beast. The hall is associated with the modern town of Lejre in Zealand (Denmark).

Heoroweard [heo ro wærd], l. 2161. Son of Hrothgar's older brother, Heorogar; bypassed for the kingship in favor of Hrothgar. Some Scandinavian legends indicate that later he killed his cousin Hrothulf (Hrolf), who had become king of the Danes, and became king himself for a very short time before being killed.

Herebeald [her bæld], ll. 2434, 2463. Eldest son of the Geat king Hrethel; slain accidentally by his brother Hæthcyn.

Heremod [her mōd], ll. 901, 1709. An early Danish king; exemplum of the bad ruler;

killed among the Jutes. Presumably it was his death that left the Danes lordless till God sent Scyld to them.

Hereric [her reek], l. 2206. Uncle of Heardred, Hyglac's son; probably the brother of Queen Hygd.

Hetware [het wār], ll. 2363, 2916. A Frankish tribe on the lower Rhine; with the Hugas and Frisians, defeated Hyglac.

Hildeburh [hil de burχ], ll. 1071, 1114. Finn's queen, sister of Hnæf (in the Finn Episode).

Hnæf [hnæf], ll. 1069, 1108, 1114. Slain leader of the Half-Danes, brother of Hildeburh (in the Finn Episode).

Hoc [hōk], l. 1076. Father of Hildeburh and Hnæf.

Hreosnabeorh [hrēōz nə beorχ], l. 2478. A hill in Geatland, site of a raid by the sons of the Swedish king Ongentheow.

Hrethel [Hrā ðl], passim. The old king of the Geats; father of Hyglac and grandfather of Beowulf; died of grief when his second son, Hæthcyn, accidentally killed his eldest son, Herebeald.

Hrethlings [hrāð lingz], l. 2960. The sons of Hrethel and, by extension, the Geats.

Hrethric [hrāð reek], ll. 1189, 1836. The elder son of King Hrothgar.

Hronesness [hron əs nes], ll. 2805, 3136. "Whale's Cliff," the headland that is the site for Beowulf's burial.

Hrothgar [hrōð gär], passim. The Danish king who built Heorot; the chief figure, apart from Beowulf, in the first part of the poem (ll. 1–2199).

Hrothmund [hrōð mund], l. 1189. The younger son of King Hrothgar.

Hrothulf [hrōð ulf], ll. 1015, 1181. Nephew of Hrothgar; joint ruler of the Danes with Hrothgar; son of Halga—see further under Heoroweard.

Hrunting [hrun ting], ll. 1457, 1490, 1659, 1807. The famous sword which Unferth lends Beowulf for his fight with Grendel's mother.

Hugas [hyū gŏs], ll. 2502, 2914. A tribe of the Franks, allied with the Hetware and the Frisians.

Hunlafing [hūn lä ving], l. 1143. A Half-Dane (in the Finn Episode), possibly the son of a slain warrior Hunlaf, brother of Guthlaf and Oslaf. But see note to text at l. 1143.

Hygd [hiyd], ll. 1926, 2172, 2369. Queen of the Geats, Hyglac's wife.

Hyglac [hiy läk], passim. Beowulf's uncle, king of the Geats; third son of Hrethel; husband of Hygd, father of Heardred; killed in A.D. 521, historical sources tell us, in his raid on the lower Rhine against the Franks and Frisians.

Ing [ing], ll. 1043, 1319. A legendary Danish king (or god).

Ingeld [ing geld], l. 2065. Son of Froda; king of the Heatho-beards; married to Hrothgar's daughter Fearwaru.

Jutes, ll. 1072, 1088, 1141, 1145. Either another name for the East Frisians ruled by Finn, or a tribe allied with them (in the Finn Episode).

Lapland, l. 580. Northern Sweden and Norway. The OE text refers here to the land of the *Finnas*, that is, Lapps.

Modthryth [mōd thrith], l. 1931. A cruel queen contrasted with the generous Hygd; after marriage to King Offa of the Angles, she became far less cruel.

Nægling [næi ling], l. 2681. Beowulf's sword in his fight with the dragon.

Offa [of fa], ll. 1949, 1957. Fourth-century king of the Angles. See note to ll. 1944–60.

Ohthere [ōχt her], ll. 2380, 2393, 2612, 2928, 2931. Son of the Swedish king Ongentheow; brother of Onela; father of Eadgils and Eanmund.

Onela [on ə lä], ll. 62, 2383, 2396, 2616, 2931. Son of the Swedish king Ongentheow, and later king himself; married to daughter of Halfdane.

Ongentheow [ong gən thāō], passim. Swedish king, father of Ohthere and Onela; he defeated and killed the Geatish king Hæthcyn near Ravenswood, and was killed in turn by Hyglac's warrior-brothers Eofor and Wulf.

Oslaf [ōz läf], l. 1148. A Half-Dane, brother of Guthlaf (in the Finn Episode).

Ravenswood, l. 2925. A forest in Sweden near where the Geatish king Hæthcyn was killed in the battle with Ongentheow's forces.

-Scyldings [shil dingz], passim. See Genealogical Tables. The Danes as a nation, descendants of Scyld; the name appears in several compounded forms.

Scyld Scefing [shild shā ving], ll. 4, 18, 27. Legendary founder of the Danish dynasty after the disastrous reign of Heremod.

-Scylfings [shil vingz], passim. See Genealogical Tables. The Swedish nation; the name appears in several compounded forms.

Sigmund [siy mund], ll. 875, 884. Son of Wæls; legendary Germanic hero—see notes to ll. 875–84 and 884–97.

Sweden, ll. 2382, 2496. The east-central part of present-day Sweden, north of the great lakes that separated the Swedes from the Geats.

Swedes, Swedish, ll. 2473, 2923, 2947, 2958, 3001. The inhabitants of Sweden, as then constituted; in particular, the Scylfings.

Swerting [swer ting], l. 1202. Hyglac's grandfather.

Unferth [un ferth], ll. 499, 530, 1165, 1488. Son of Ecglaf; Hrothgar's thyle—see note to ll. 1164–65; challenger of Beowulf concerning his swimming match with Breca.

Vandals, l. 348. The tribe to which Wulfgar belongs; probably to be associated with Vendel, in Sweden

Wægmundings [wæi mun dingz], ll. 2607, 2814. The family to which both Beowulf and Wiglaf belong.

Wæls [wælz], l. 875. Father of Sigmund.

Wealhtheow [wælχ thāō], passim. Hrothgar's Queen; mother of Hrethric and Hrothmund.

Weders [we dərz], passim. The Geats.

Weland [wā lənd], l. 455. Legendary Germanic smith.

Weohstan [wāōχ stän], passim. Father of Wiglaf; slayer of Eanmund. See note to ll. 2602–3 on tribal affiliations.

Wiglaf [wiy läf], passim. Beowulf's thane and kinsman, who helps him kill the dragon; son of Weohstan; a Wægmunding.

Withergild [wi ðər gild], l. 2051. A Heatho-beard, slain in the feud with the Danes.

Wonred [won rād], ll. 2964, 2971. Father of Eofor and Wulf, the Geatish brothers who killed Ongentheow.

Wulf [wulf], ll. 2964, 2992. Son of Wonred, brother of Eofor; first to wound Ongentheow, but severely wounded in turn by that old Swedish king.

Wulfgar [wulf gär], ll. 348, 360. Hrothgar's hall-warden, herald, and officer.

Wylfings [wil vingz], ll. 461, 471. A Germanic tribe, probably located south of the Baltic.

Yrmenlaf [ir mən läf], l. 1324. Younger brother of Hrothgar's counselor Ashere.

List of Poetic Translators

Francis B. Gummere (1909)
John R. Clark Hall (1914)
C. K. Scott Moncrieff (1921)
William Ellery Leonard (1923)
Archibald Strong (1925)
D. H. Crawford (1926)
G. H. Gerould (1929)
Charles W. Kennedy (1940)
Gavin Bone (1945)
Mary E. Waterhouse (1949)
Edwin Morgan (1952)
Burton Raffel (1963)
Kevin Crossley-Holland (1968)
Michael Alexander (1973)
Howell D. Chickering, Jr. (1977)

Selected Bibliography

Bibliographies

Fry, Donald K. *"Beowulf" and "The Fight at Finnsburh": A Bibliography*. Charlottesville: The Univ. Pr. of Virginia, 1969.

Greenfield, Stanley B., and Fred C. Robinson. *A Bibliography of Publications on Old English Literature to the End of 1972*. Toronto: Univ. of Toronto Pr., 1980.

Short, Douglas D. *"Beowulf" Scholarship: An Annotated Bibliography*. New York: Garland Pub. Co., 1980.

Editions

Klaeber, Friedrich. *"Beowulf" and "The Fight at Finnsburg."* 3rd ed. Boston: Heath, 1950.

Wrenn, C. L. *"Beowulf," with the Finnesburg Fragment*. 2nd ed. London: Harrap, 1958. Rev. ed. edited by Whitney F. Bolton, 1973.

Translations

See List of Poetic Translators.

Studies

Bonjour, Adrien. *The Digressions in "Beowulf."* Oxford: Blackwell, 1950.

Brodeur, Arthur G. *The Art of "Beowulf."* Berkeley: Univ. of California Pr., 1959.

Goldsmith, Margaret E. *The Mode and Meaning of "Beowulf."* London: Athlone Pr., 1970.

Haarder, Andreas. *"Beowulf": The Appeal of a Poem.* Copenhagen: Akademisk Forlag, 1975.

Irving, Edward B., Jr. *A Reading of "Beowulf."* New Haven: Yale Univ. Pr., 1968.

Shippey, Thomas A. *Beowulf.* London, Edward Arnold, 1978.

Sisam, Kenneth. *The Structure of "Beowulf."* Oxford: Clarendon Pr., 1965.

Collections of Essays

Fry, Donald K. *The "Beowulf" Poet.* Englewood Cliffs, N.J.: Prentice-Hall, 1968.

Nicholson, Lewis E. *An Anthology of "Beowulf" Criticism.* Notre Dame: Univ. of Notre Dame Pr., 1963.

Tuso, Joseph F. *"Beowulf: The Donaldson Translation, Backgrounds and Sources, Criticism.* New York: Norton, 1975.

Backgrounds

Chambers, R. W. *"Beowulf": An Introduction*. 3rd ed., with Supplement by C. L. Wrenn. Cambridge: Cambridge Univ. Pr., 1959.

Garmonsway, G. N., Jacqueline Simpson, and Hilda Ellis Davidson. *"Beowulf" and Its Analogues*. London: Dent, 1968.

Watts, Ann C. *The Lyre and the Harp*. New Haven: Yale Univ. Pr., 1969.

Whitelock, Dorothy. *The Audience of "Beowulf."* Oxford: Clarendon Pr., 1951.

STANLEY B. GREENFIELD, a leading Anglo-Saxon scholar, is Professor of English, University of Oregon. Feeling a need for a readable version of *Beowulf* that would capture the imagination of today's general reader and student, Greenfield here provides an accurate and aesthetically satisfying poetic translation of the Old English epic. Among the translator's numerous publications are *A Critical History of Old English Literature* (1965), *The Interpretation of Old English Poems* (1972), and, with Fred C. Robinson, *A Bibliography of Publications on Old English Literature to the End of 1972* (1980).

ALAIN RENOIR, author of the Introduction to this volume, is Professor of English, University of California, Berkeley. He has published widely on Old English and other medieval literatures, and is an authority on oral-formulaic theory and critical application of it to those literatures.